Design City
TORONTO

Other Wiley Editorial Offices

John Wiley & Sons Inc., 111 River Street, Hoboken, NJ 07030, USA

Jossey-Bass, 989 Market Street, San Francisco, CA 94103-1741, USA

Wiley-VCH Verlag GmbH, Boschstr. 12, D-69469 Weinheim, Germany

John Wiley & Sons Australia Ltd, 42 McDougall Street, Milton, Queensland
    4064, Australia

John Wiley & Sons (Asia) Pte Ltd, 2 Clementi Loop #02-01, Jin Xing
    Distripark, Singapore 129809

John Wiley & Sons Canada Ltd, 5353 Dundas Street West, Suite 400,
    Etobicoke, Ontario M9B 6H8, Canada

Wiley also publishes its books in a variety of electronic formats. Some
content that appears in print may not be available in electronic books.

Executive Commissioning Editor: Helen Castle
Content Editor: Louise Porter
Publishing Assistant: Calver Lezama

ISBN 978 0 470 033166

Cover design by Jennifer Flores and Ian Lambot Studio, UK
Page design and layouts by Ian Lambot Studio, UK
Printed and bound in Canada

Design City
TORONTO

Sean Stanwick and **Jennifer Flores**
photography by **Tom Arban**

Foreword by **Daniel Libeskind**

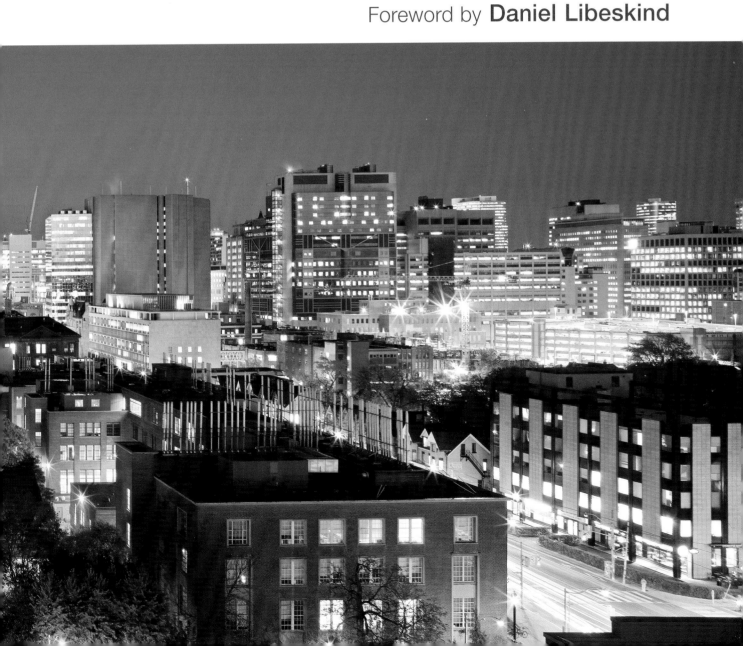

Contents

Preface

When our publisher first posed the question, 'Is Toronto a *Design City*?' we knew instinctively that it was. Toronto is experiencing a renaissance, as socially and architecturally, our cultural spaces take on new prominence. Living and working in the city, we can see the high rate of construction, especially in the downtown core, where the erecting of new buildings and the renovations of old are a daily sight. Yet we know that to be a *Design City*, there needs to be more than just beautifully designed spaces. Design exists in many forms – in the chaos of signage lining Chinatown streets; in the rhythmic patterns of commuters moving in and out of the subway tunnels; in the reflections of cars whizzing by the glass facades of shiny towers. For us, a *Design City* exists when city dwellers and tourists, the design educated and the design buffs alike can all equally see and appreciate the beauty of design in the city around them.

While we felt there was a need for a book that celebrated this wonderful time in the architectural story of our city, what confirmed it was a conversation we had with a friend. Looking at a picture of Will Alsop's Sharp Centre for Design, she questioned, 'Is *that* in Toronto?' Over and over again, that scenario repeated itself as friends and family were surprised by the projects found within the pages of this book. These were people who had lived here their whole lives yet had never seen nor even known these spaces existed.

This book was never envisioned as an analytical discourse on architectural theory or a thorough dissection of the Toronto style, nor was it written to be a tourist guidebook. We hope it resides somewhere in between, as a book that presents an approachable and personal architecture enjoyed equally by residents and tourists alike. Our photographer Tom Arban has given you one view onto the city; his pictures capture a Toronto that is alive and thriving, colourful, and optimistic about what lies ahead. We invite you to explore this city, consciously. In our interview with him, Daniel Libeskind said it best: 'Architecture at its deepest sense is about creating space that has never been there, and giving people a kind of vista … as if one would see the city in a very different way through this new space.'

We hope this book helps you to see Toronto as it is – truly, a *Design City*.

Foreword

Great cities have always been associated with great architecture. More than that, architecture has formed the substance, image, and uniqueness of each city. There are times when a palpable shift, a seismic urban energy, catapults a city to a new level. Whether it is eighteenth-century Paris or early twentieth-century New York, there is a moment in which a city's form emerges.

When I lived in Toronto in the early 1970s the city was eminently liveable, but outside vibrant neighbourhoods, the striking City Hall, and the memorable Mies towers, architecture was generally undistinguished. This is certainly no longer true. Suddenly, seemingly only in the past five years, the city is exploding with new and exciting architecture. There is a new horizon that has opened up – in a sense, we are what we look at. We are what we live in. We are what we aspire to. And what this new Toronto aspires to is an architecture that is as exciting as its culture, is as varied as its diversity, and is as open as the youthful minds that flood the streets.

What makes a renaissance? A renaissance is a connection between *what the city was* and *what the city can be*. This discovery entails digging deeper into possibilities. At the same time, it challenges architecture and planning to take risks because what is to be built is more than just 'one more building'. The renaissance implies bringing back the wonder of architecture to the public at large by breaking free from the straitjacket of 'this is how our city has always been'. The breaking of formulas, the challenge of building something that has never been built before, the daring that goes with originality – all these speak of a new sense of identity for a city. A dynamic development, such as the renaissance of architecture in Toronto, renews more than street fronts … it explodes the myth that stereotypes 'Toronto The Good', suddenly making it 'Toronto The Great'.

Daniel Libeskind
November 2006

Cities don't change gradually, they change suddenly... and this is one of those moments. There was a period of inertia in Toronto where there was little happening in design and architecture and suddenly there was a kind of energy reflecting a desire for architecture and design to be part of people's lives. It's a very special period... a real renaissance.

Daniel Libeskind interview with the Authors
Toronto – June 2006

Introduction

The New City Space

Whether you are an architect, an interior designer or simply a city dweller, it is almost impossible not to notice the large amount of construction that is currently underway within Toronto. With so many culture-based building projects all happening at once, it is without a doubt an exciting time to be in the city. Call it Hogtown, Toronto the Good, Design City, or even Torontopia, whatever moniker you choose, the City of Toronto, as we know it will be forever changed. Affectionately dubbed the city's architectural renaissance, the building boom has actually grown beyond bricks and mortar to include large-scale urban design projects, cultural initiatives, and even philosophical enlightenment as people's attitudes towards architecture and the city have grown more sophisticated.

Interestingly, the renewal effort has itself become a homespun media-darling as newspapers, websites, chat rooms and blogs are continually abuzz with news of the changing space and face of the city. Five years ago, it would have been inconceivable to the local design community that the world's most important architectural practitioners including Frank Gehry, Daniel Libeskind, Lord Norman Foster and Will Alsop would each be working here at the same time. Somehow, the impossible has happened and Toronto is now knee-deep in a phenomenal act of city (re)making. If a renaissance is about rebirth and enlightenment, then Toronto's architectural renaissance is certainly on its way to maturity.

Riding this wave of renewal is a number of significant and well-respected cultural institutions and when complete, they will have contributed to the largest renewal of the city's cultural infrastructure in decades. British architect Will Alsop has completed the first step with his perilous Sharp Centre for Design (the Tabletop) at the Ontario College of Art and Design (OCAD). At the hands of Frank Gehry the Art Gallery of Ontario (AGO) will undergo a massive internal renovation and facelift, while New York architect Daniel Libeskind is remaking, in the form of crystalline gems, another grand dame of the city, the Royal Ontario Museum (ROM). At the University of Toronto campus, Britain's Lord Norman Foster has delivered his first Canadian work for the pharmacy faculty, with a refined glass lantern that shrouds two suspended ovoid pods within the lobby. And next door, Stuttgart's Behnisch Architekten gives the city a lesson in sustainability at the Terrence Donnelly Centre for Cellular and Biomolecular Research, which features a unique double skin of glass and internal bamboo gardens.

While we revel in the arrival of star architects and marvel at their creations, Canadians are unfortunately often timid when it comes to lauding the creative talents of our own and flaunting their skills on the international stage. This is why *Design City Toronto* is even more relevant in order to celebrate the city's local talent. As the spotlight is aimed squarely at international star architects, we must not forget that Toronto is, and has been for many years, a creative design city capable of producing architecture that is historically on a par with that of our North American and even European contemporaries.

The city's modern architectural legacy runs deep thanks largely to the enthusiasm of architectural pioneers John B and John C Parkin and Peter Dickinson who, throughout the 1950s and 1960s, would translate their enthusiasm for

Above
The advanced Terrence Donnelly Centre for Cellular and Biomolecular Research sits within Toronto's Discovery District, one of the most concentrated clusters of research and medical institutions worldwide

Canadian design into their own style of modernism that emphasised simplicity and a respect for the local vernacular.[1] The Parkins' ecru-brick Salvation Army building (now demolished) and their stainless-steel Sun Life Building on University Avenue were both solid examples that served to galvanise the modernist language in the city core. Today, noted architectural firms like Diamond and Schmitt, Kuwabara Payne McKenna Blumberg, and Montgomery Sisam carry on with a similar style that is both highly modern but also sympathetic to the city's rich architectural fabric.

Several interior designers are also helping fuel the renaissance. With a passion for the slightly schizophrenic, 3rd UNCLE design makes innovative use of found objects at The Drake Hotel to create an ad-hoc collage of textures and intellectual-kitsch, while munge//leung (who trained at the hip of Yabu Pushelberg, the Canadian design darlings responsible for W New York and Tiffany's Fifth Avenue), use a rich material palette to create warm and inviting spaces for Ultra Supper Club and then switch gears into retro-chic colours and translucent plastics for Lux, a trendy dinner lounge in the city's west end.

Design City Toronto celebrates, in approachable yet informative terms, many of these designers and their work. It is by no means a comprehensive manuscript on the history of modern architecture in Toronto, nor is it solely a tourist guidebook. Instead, *Design City Toronto* intentionally chooses to reside somewhere in between the two, in the space explored by architects, interior designers, tourists, the design-curious and urban dwellers alike. Very much like the architecture that makes up the city's urban fabric, *Design City Toronto* is a hybrid, examining the city from multiple kaleidoscopic view cones. Spawned by the need to capture this unique moment in time, its true hope is simply to inspire a refreshing reacquaintance with our city.

The projects featured in this book, over thirty in all, are organised around four central themes. The first chapter, 'discover*Explore*' recognises that creativity is ingrained deep within the soul of the city and as such, highlights a number of cultural projects including the ROM, the AGO and the Young Centre for Performing Arts. The second chapter, 'eat*Enjoy*' explores several popular restaurants that reflect both the breadth of cuisine and the depth of creative talent available. Chapter three, 'relax*Recharge*' proves that city dwellers can find an abundance of choice in their search for rest and relaxation. Projects featured range from the retro-chic Drake Hotel

Above
Known as an *izakaya*, a red lantern
hanging outside the door of a restaurant
typically means an inexpensive hot
meal, a spot for casual drinks and an
informal atmosphere

Below
British architect Will Alsop, designer of
the new Sharp Centre for Design at the
Ontario College of Art & Design

to a divine convent in the city's north end. The fourth chapter, 'learn*Study*' shows
how university and private learning spaces such as Canada's National Ballet School
and the Schulich School of Business, can be vehicles for testing new ideas both in
terms of teaching and city building. The book also features an informative narrative of
the city's rich urban neighbourhoods from The Beach to Parkdale.

Design City Toronto

What does it mean to be labelled with the moniker *Design City*? Is Toronto a *Design
City*? Will Alsop suggested that Toronto is experiencing an exotic change, as we are
designing a history that the city never had.[2] Is this the criteria: the ability to create
history and the future of a city at the same time? Or is it the ability of a metropolis
to import the world's best brand-name designers and architects to create globally
recognised iconic works?

 If these are the measures, then the arrival of Daniel Libeskind, Lord Norman
Foster and Frank Gehry who are collectively shaping the future space of the city must
surely be evidence enough of Toronto's *Design City* status. But, while attracting star
talent from abroad certainly adds cachet, it fails to credit local talent, which in this
city's case has been a driving force in developing its neo-modern architectural style.
Or is a *Design City* one that is simply experiencing its 'fifteen minutes' of fame, as was
the case in Bilbao Spain when Frank Gehry seduced the world with his Guggenheim
Museum? Perhaps this is the case, however, it is unlikely that Toronto will receive the
same international media fervour that landed on Bilbao.

 Might it also be the result of curatorial examinations? If so, Toronto's
architecture has been the subject of several significant exhibitions throughout its life,
including the recent display at the AGO, which showcased several cultural projects
currently under renovation, or the 1987 exhibition *Toronto Le Nouveau Nouveau*

Monde, curated by architect Ruth Cawker, which examined twenty influential modern projects within the city core.

Likely though, the best measure is simply that to be a *Design City* there should be an acknowledgment of the value of design, and that the results must be pervasive across building types, communities and genres. To this measure, Toronto can easily lay claim to its *Design City* status.

One need only look around to see that the renaissance is contagious and not limited to singular iconic buildings. Of course, private patronage for these cultural projects is also at an all time high with massive donations in both money and art. Embracing our industrial heritage, the abandoned Brick Works will soon morph from a derelict industrial site to a working sustainable discovery centre. Nascent fires have been lit yet again on our Waterfront Revitalisation Initiative. Led by local design firm du Toit Allsopp Hillier and Rotterdam's West 8, the city may finally realise the full potential of the waterfront. Even healthcare projects, such as the Wellesley Central Place by Farrow Partnership Architects, are embracing a more humanistic attitude toward design incorporating wood, courtyards and green roofs. There is even growing interest in simply living in the city as a number of residential condominium projects are currently under construction within the core including a project by Donald Trump who has lent his name to a deluxe hotel and residential tower.

Culture City Toronto

While Toronto is certainly beginning to look the part of a *Design City*, the question remains does it have the character to go with its new suit? The short answer is yes. Toronto is without a doubt, a creative city on a par with global contemporary metropolises such as Chicago, Milan, Montreal, New York and San Francisco. What enables us to lay claim to being Canada's creative capital is the simple fact that the city supports over 25 per cent of the nation's creative industry jobs.[3] We also place great value on creativity as a means to secure our identity within the country; the city's creative machinery generates over eight billion in revenue annually and accounts for over half of the Province's cultural revenues.[4] Additionally, Toronto is the most visited tourist destination in the country, welcoming over 18 million visitors annually, and to the tourists, participating in one of the many cultural attractions is second only to shopping.[5] We are also a city of great cuisines with an increasingly sophisticated palate. In short, today's Toronto is a veritable menu of cultural choices.

Not only is the city undergoing a broad sweeping architectural renaissance, as over a dozen significant cultural institutions, public and private are being transformed, we are also in the midst of a great cultural revival. Blogs posted on the Reading Cities[6] website, an open forum devoted to the city's current urban and architectural design issues, are abuzz with discussions by some of the city's most noted designers

Above
Wellesley Central Place. Even healthcare projects, like this long-term care facility in Cabbagetown by Farrow Partnership Architects, embrace a sustainable mandate and feature sunshades and 'green' roofs

Right
The Gardiner Museum of Ceramic Art contains more than 2900 pieces, including the world's most impressive cache of European pottery and porcelain from the 15th to the 19th centuries

and cultural mavens. The *[murmur]* project is an independent initiative that offers on-location, on-demand audio podcasts of significant architectural and cultural moments around the city. The annual Doors Open architectural tour, where well over a hundred normally private buildings, offices and residences open their doors to the public, is growing exponentially, while the annual Toronto International Film Festival is widely recognised as the world's largest film festival by attendance. The city also recently announced its newest summer arts festival. Titled Luminato, the event will showcase the best of Canadian and international artists over a 10-day period in June 2007.

Sponsored by the municipal government, a number of public initiatives are also investigating the role of culture, creativity and architecture in shaping the future city. The Live with Culture[7] campaign is a 16-month grassroots celebration of the arts at various venues across the city. On an economic note, the recently published *Strategies for Creative Cities*[8] project and the *Culture Plan for a Creative City 2003* both recognised that architecture could be a valuable asset in a broader tourism and economic action plan for the city.

Toronto is also home to a great cultural diversity within its borders. Like many, the city has undergone several waves of immigration with the Italians in the 1950s, the Greeks in 1970s and most recently, the Asians. This breadth of diversity is deeply rooted and reflected in the various neighbourhoods through local street festivals such as Greektown's Taste of the Danforth and Little Italy's Corso Italia Toronto Fiesta in July. In a city where over 100 languages are spoken ever day, culture is clearly at the core of our city building initiative. With access to a high quality of life, environment, healthcare and education, it is no wonder that the Toronto is consistently rated as one of the most liveable cities in the world.[9]

Birth of a Renaissance

No doubt the waves of cultural and civic change are infectious and spreading throughout the city, but the interesting discussion really centres on (if we borrow a term from author Malcolm Gladwell) the 'tipping point'[10] that inspired this renaissance in the first place.

Often we are tempted to look for specific causes to major events. While there are some manic examples that appear to have single-handedly spawned the building boom, Toronto's renaissance should be likened more to raindrops in a pond, each creating their own singular ripple, spreading and colliding with each other to create a collective up-swell of enthusiasm and energy. But what are these raindrops?

One could easily argue that the arrival of Daniel Libeskind at the Royal Ontario Museum (ROM) was the first. But predating the ROM by two years is Alsop's fantastical Tabletop at the OCAD. Perched precariously atop colourful stilts, the pixelated white box has rightfully earned its place as the new and definitive iconic image of the city. If iconicity is the measure, the discussion must look back to 2001 and Graduate House, a graduate student residence at the University of Toronto designed by local architect Stephen Teeple and Californian deconstructivist Thom Mayne of Morphosis. Brazenly invading the quiet space of the street, Graduate House single-handedly launched a long overdue debate on city making. One might also place credit in the hands of two of the city's cultural mavens, late media mogul Ken Thomson and ROM Director William Thorsell. Each were vital in their individual promotions of the value and necessity of bringing a star architect to Toronto; Thomson brought Frank Gehry home to the AGO while Thorsell raised the public awareness of the ROM by securing Libeskind through an open international competition.

But architecture cannot do the job alone. Many of the cultural projects underway, including the ROM, would not have even broken ground without the Provincial Government's SuperBuild endowment fund. Pouring over CA$20 billion into the Province's infrastructure, the growth fund is the largest single injection of public sector monies in decades. Additionally, private patronage is a significant driving force as philanthropic donors have contributed over CA$900 million to the city building initiative.

For all its support, the next question perhaps is not what started the renaissance, but rather will it last? While one could posit that this is the city's 'fifteen

Above
For the international open competiton to build the Graduate House, the mandate was clear: the university was seeking a 'landmark' gateway project

minutes of fame', obviously there is hope that the momentum will continue and that this new and existing infrastructure will sustain long-term urban growth. Whether Torontonians carry on is uncertain, but there is optimism in Daniel Libeskind's words:

I hope that Toronto will... continue to express itself and develop itself in design, architecture, and every other way, socially as well, to be what it is: one of the great world cities. It's not just a provincial city, its really part of the world. And now, I think it will become more and more one of the destinations in the world, where if you live in Paris or you live in Tokyo, you will come to Toronto because it's an important city to visit, to be in, to enjoy.[11]

A Toronto Vernacular

While some cities can be immediately associated with a singular style or attitude toward design, such as Tokyo for its wild neonism, or Chicago as the birthplace of the skyscraper, defining a uniform Toronto style is indeed a complex distillation process. A relatively new city, having only risen as a contemporary metropolis in the post-war years, Toronto is split between a conflicted desire to endorse itself as a modern *Design City*, and its ingrained connection with our Anglo-Victorian small-town heritage; paradoxically evidenced by its ability to attract star architects such as Foster or Gehry, and the longevity of the annual agrarian Royal Agricultural Winter Fair.

Part of the difficulty also stems from the city's vast cultural diversity as a wealth of ingrained perceptions and values continually percolate through to create the rich

Right
At the Schulich School of Business, the adjacent woodlot and three landscaped courtyards provide a sense of calm and refuge from the bustle of campus life

and versatile palette of textures, materials and shapes that define our built fabric. This diversity can actually be seen as both a curse and a panacea. While it fosters the lack of a distinct style, to its credit, this same diversity gives the city the ability to absorb a variety of radical architectural themes. So if one were to attempt to extract a quintessential Toronto style, two fundamental streams of thought begin to emerge.

On one hand, the design renaissance has clearly created a newfound desire for the *iconic* spectacle. Architect Daniel Libeskind suggested that what is truly important is the spirit of the city, and that because of a revolution in our expectations for architecture Toronto will never be the same again.[12] We believe he is right. History has shown that extreme architecture was something the city once feared. The excess of 1970s prosaic bunker-like buildings, which still plague the city, are a salient example of our architectural timidity. Yet, as the collective momentum to have our built spaces better reflect our cosmopolitan demographic grows, and as the ebb of the renaissance sweeps away our design trepidation, we are now also easily seduced by star architects and their manic architectural moments.

In the span of just five short years, we have become the new consumer of iconic architecture and now entertain buildings that were once considered far too radical for our puritan interpretations of the space of the city. Where we once sat aghast at the sight of Stephen Teeple's Graduate House with its cantilevered steel marquee and asked 'is that in Toronto?' Today that very same question is posed not in disgust, but instead in excitement as we revel in the uniqueness of Alsop's precarious Tabletop. We now expect exploding sculptural gestures from Gehry; we eagerly anticipate Libeskind's crystalline blocks, and in fact are disappointed to find that not all crystals are transparent. That these architects will create something unique in our city, something that the world will stand up and take notice of is now a basic expectation. And though not always met with uniform welcome, these projects have been lauded as key progenitors of Toronto's rebirth as a *Design City*.

Though some may pine for the ebullient fluidity of Frank Gehry, on the other hand, ours is also a style of the 'gentleman architect'; a version of good-mannered, parochial neo-modernism that (perhaps paradoxically) bridges the gap between nature and the machine thus connecting the agrarian hamlet of the past with the modern city of the future.

Throughout the 1950s, modernist architecture in Toronto manifested itself in a very unique and specific manner. While many local architects welcomed the functional, pragmatic aspects of The International Style, we also refused to embrace modernism's machine aesthetic carte blanche, choosing instead to consider context and history as equally valuable and necessary elements in the broader process of city making. In essence, our buildings were both *of* and *for* the city, respecting the neighbourhood and the lives of its inhabitants rather than forcing its own design agenda upon them.

Some 50 years on, this mindset still prevails. It is quite ironic that Toronto is in the midst of its largest building boom since the 1950s and yet this city somehow managed to tame Frank Gehry into delivering not a shimmering blob, but rather a shimmering titanium box for the AGO. Nevertheless, a direct line can be traced between Toronto's early modernism, such as Mies Van der Rohe's 1967 iconic TD Banking Centre, and the highly-contextual neo-modern projects being constructed today, such as the new Opera House by Diamond and Schmitt, Canada's National Ballet School by Kuwabara Payne McKenna Blumberg or the Schulich School of Business at York University by Hariri Pontarini Architects. We can also look to the new

Above
Wrapping itself asymmetrically around
three sides, the crisp transparent wings
of Canada's National Ballet School form
a shimmering backdrop for the textured
ecru brick and restored cornice moulding of historic Northfield House

Below
With clean lines and plenty of glass the
Four Seasons Centre for the Performing
Arts is a perfect example of the refined
modernism that has become synony-
mous with the Toronto style

works by Sir Norman Foster (Leslie L Dan Pharmacy Building) and Behnisch
Architekten (Terrence Donnelly Centre for Cellular and Biomolecular Research) at the
University of Toronto campus. While both firms are known for their contemporary
designs, both have delivered very Toronto-esque adaptations of the modern glass
box. Ultimately though, by embracing the conservatism of pre-war Toronto, several
local design firms have helped ensure the longevity of the quintessential Toronto neo-
modern vernacular.

The Old Modern

Compared with its European and even North American counterparts, modernism
came late to Toronto. As New Yorkers and Chicagoans were revelling in the technical
marvel of their steel skyscrapers, Torontonians were happy to go about their day
amidst rows of stone and brick Victorian buildings on tree-lined avenues.

But, in the years following the Second World War and with the nation's victory
in Europe, Toronto was a vibrant city of energy and confidence. The 1950s saw a
great economic and building boom that brought with it a progressive outlook on city
building. Industrial designers such as Fred Moffat, graphic designers, potters and
weavers collectively defined the Canadian style with household products that would
enrich and sustain our newfound modern lifestyle. Artists Jack Bush and Michael
Snow would stir the nation awake from its parochial values with their inspirational
visions. In fact, so elated were we by the burgeoning post-war economy that we even
branded our factories (eg the 'Victory' Soya Mills at the water's edge) and they
became symbols of the city's new industrial supremacy.[13]

In this period, Toronto was the hotbed of modernism and its style was fresh and
full of vigour. During this heyday several influential designers, including Peter
Dickinson, and father and son team John B and John C Parkin, would set up shop
in the burgeoning city and create a legacy of spin-off firms, some of which are still
around today – for example Page and Steele, and WZMH (Webb Zerafa Menkes
Housden). Through their use of precast and poured-in-place concrete, aluminium

curtain walls, metal sash windows and polished terrazzo flooring; these energetic firms would forge the quintessential Toronto modern aesthetic.[14] One of the early projects that shifted the balance in favour of contemporary modern architecture would be the design for the Ontario Association of Architects headquarters by John B Parkin. Its low-slung horizontal bands of brick and glass tucked themselves effortlessly into the ravine hillside and still remain an iconic example for architects in the city. Toronto was also home to Don Mills, the first post-war large-scale residential community planned by private developers. Conceived more as a garden city than a traditional suburb, Don Mills was a testing ground for a number of innovative planning concepts including a centralized shopping centre flanked by four residential quadrants each knit together by a continuous greenbelt.

Ultimately though, the single project that would tip the scales was the international competition for the New City Hall and Civic Square (later renamed Nathan Phillips Square) awarded to Finnish architect Viljo Revell in 1958. From a jury led by international architects Eero Saarinen and Ernesto Rogers, the crescent sculptural concrete forms that wrapped a futuristic white pod forced the city to embrace its modern, democratic future. In fact, so confident was the design community that many international architects uprooted and came to the city to establish practices.

Throughout the late 1960s and early '70s Toronto moved into a somewhat heroic period seeing a greater commitment to more generic and monolithic structures. Of course, the greatest legacies of this era are the 1967 Toronto Dominion Centre by Mies van der Rohe (with Bregman and Hamann and John B Parkin), the Toronto Eaton Centre and the waterfront theme park, Ontario Place, by Zeidler Partnership. Australian architect John Andrews, who was placed second to Revell in the City Hall competition, also created the mammoth CN Tower, the tallest freestanding structure in the world during this period. Raymond Moriyama would also begin his lengthy career with the slightly brutalist concrete Ontario Science Centre that terraced itself deep into a ravine.

The New Modern

As in many North American cities, the onslaught of modernism in the late 1970s and onward, brought with it a blanket disregard for older, outmoded architecture that resulted in the uniform razing of vast tracts of Toronto's urban and largely historic neighbourhoods and its grand boulevards. Rallying against the real (and perceived) destructive effects of a brutal modernism a number of local architects, with support from prominent urban theorist Jane Jacobs, resisted and invested their efforts back into the city core with innovative infill projects that preserved and intensified the existing and fast disappearing urban fabric.

Above
There is a growing interest in simply living in the city, as demonstrated by the number of condominium projects currently being completed in the vacant waterfront lands adjacent the Rogers Centre (Skydome) and the CN Tower

Below
At Canada's National Ballet School the design sensitivity integrates old and new buildings as an ensemble of dance training, academic and residential facilities

Early in their careers, architects Jack Diamond and Barton Myers each explored a number of high-density, low-rise courtyard prototypes such as York Square (1968) and Hydro Block Housing (1975). Equally important was architect George Baird who advocated for urban renewal by way of podium and arcade additions to existing towers, although Baird was never able to realise a completed prototype.[15] Nevertheless, by integrating existing neighbourhood streets and preserving the historic building stock, Diamond, Myers, and Baird were each able to establish standards for urban design, many of which the city still adopts today.

Toronto modernism, for the most part, has consistently sought an architectural and stylistic unification between contemporary industrial materials and traditional values and ideologies; an approach that has enabled several contemporary design firms to flourish. Leading the pack are the progeny of the original firm of Diamond and Myers: the present day Diamond and Schmitt Architects, and Kuwabara Payne McKenna Blumberg (KPMB). Throughout their careers, each have taken the lessons learned from their mentorship at Diamond and Myers, and continued to produce designs that are adventurous, but also of a style that the general public can easily understand and support.

Collectively these two firms have become the catalyst for developing an architectural legacy within the city through a modest style that is both transparent and outward looking, modern and contextual. While any number of their projects will prove the point, one need only look at how the new Four Seasons Opera House (Diamond and Schmitt Architects) sits politely on its major urban artery, or examine the way Canada's National Ballet School (KPMB) integrates with the existing heritage structures to realise that the act of unification between the existing fabric and a desire for building anew has been achieved.

What drives these two firms, and ultimately the Toronto style, is a simple notion of legibility and a sympathetic response to the unique particularities of the site. What you won't find in their portfolios, however, are iconic spectacles such as the Tabletop or Graduate House, as both Jack Diamond and Bruce Kuwabara vehemently disapprove of signature building simply for the sake of challenging the standing civic rule. For Diamond and Kuwabara, Toronto's beauty lies in the sameness of its unassuming architecture and the uniformity of its street grid. For them, and equally many other contemporary design firms in the city, it is this continuity of the urban fabric that ultimately acts as an invisible hand supporting and nurturing the city's great diversity and that will continue to provide a stable, albeit not 'spectacular' framework for future designers.

1   John Martins-Manteiga. *Mean City: From Architecture to Design: How Toronto went Boom!,* Dominion Modern, Toronto, 2005.
2   Will Alsop, interview with the authors, Toronto, June 2006.
3   Meric Gertler. *Strategies for Creative Cities: Imagine a Toronto*, a report presented by the Creative Cities Leadership Team for the Strategies for Creative Cities Project, Toronto, 2006.
4   Teitelbaum, Matthew. *Reading Cities Toronto*, www.readingcities.com, 2005.
5   www.livewithculture.ca
6   www.readingcities.com
7   www.livewithculture.ca
8   Meric Gertler. *op cit.*
9   As rated by the Economist Intelligence Unit, part of the Economist Group, a research and advisory company providing country, industry and management analysis worldwide.
10 Malcolm Gladwell. *The Tipping Point*, Little, Brown & Company, London, 2002.
11 Daniel Libeskind, interview with the authors, Toronto, June 2006.
12 *Ibid.*
13 John Martins-Manteiga. *op cit.*
14 Oscar Riera Ojeda (ed). *The Architecture of Kuwabara Payne McKenna Blumberg*, Birkhäuser Verlag, Berlin and Boston, 2004.
15 *Ibid.*

Toronto can be characterised as a fusion of culture, attitude and a desire to discover and explore. Perhaps the 2006 Poet Laureate of Toronto, Pier Giorgio Di Cicco, described it best when he wrote, 'Creativity owns imagination. And imagination is what builds our cities … This is what makes a city great'.[1]

With one out of every four creative industry jobs in the country situated in Toronto,[2] and welcoming over 18 million tourists annually, it could easily be argued that the city is fast becoming the country's nexus for arts and culture. So, as momentum for the city's unprecedented architectural renaissance grows, it is no surprise that over a dozen major cultural institutions, both public and private, are being rejuvenated and transformed. From delicate crystals at the brawny Royal Ontario Museum, to decaying brownfield relics that are finding new life as green gems in their own right, to an opera at the new Four Seasons Centre whose clean lines and glazed facade is a perfect example of the respectful modernism that has become synonymous with the Toronto style; the projects highlighted in this chapter express what most Torontonians already know: that the quality of life in this city is due largely to a collective commitment to the arts.

discover
Explore

With a critical mass of projects well under way, these institutions collectively have the power to dramatically alter the physical fabric of the city. Garnering the spotlight are the two most prominent: the Royal Ontario Museum (ROM) and the Art Gallery of Ontario (AGO). With its swooping glass scrim that slants and twists, the AGO represents not just modern architecture, but also the long overdue homecoming of the world's most famous architect, Frank Gehry. Equally engaging is the Crystal, Daniel Libeskind's vision for the ROM; his interlocking crystalline cubes will undoubtedly change the way we view and experience our city. And Libeskind agrees: 'I think it will be the experience of wonderment. People will see the city in a very different way through this new space … They will see it as what it is, a great city with incredibly interesting history'.[3]

A number of smaller private galleries and theatres are also making significant cultural inroads. Local architects Kuwabara Payne McKenna Blumberg have designed a sophisticated gem at the Gardiner Museum of Ceramic Art where a series of limestone and glass 'jewel-boxes' stack themselves up and out to form a very mature addition to an already prominent urban artery. Not far away, the Bata Shoe Museum by Moriyama and Teshima completes museum row and, like a piece of skilfully folded origami, delivers a unique knife-cut aesthetic with calculated canted walls that align with the diurnal path of the sun to create a shadow-dance on the facade. At the Young Centre for the Performing Arts, the progeny of a special partnership between George Brown College and the Soulpepper Theatre Company, patrons can enjoy local theatre set within the backdrop of the restored nineteenth-century Gooderham & Worts Distillery District.

Urban design and eco-tourism are also key aspects in the city's archi-cultural agenda. Leading the charge is local environmental group Evergreen with their project at the derelict Toronto Brick Works. Celebrating the verdant ravines and the city's industrial heyday, this

delicate merging of brick warehouses and regenerated natural wetlands will offer interactive education on the role of nature in creating livable cities. Though Toronto is still timid when it comes to large-scale urban design projects, Rotterdam landscape architect Adriaan Geuze of West 8 is also changing the space of our city as we are finally taking action on our nascent two-kilometre Waterfront Revitalisation Initiative.

While each of these influential projects owes a great deal to the Provincial Government's multibillion-dollar SuperBuild endowment fund, the city's renaissance is about more than just fantastical architecture as a number of creative-based initiatives are percolating to the surface. One of the most innovative projects is [murmur], an on-demand audio experience that recounts personal and historical narratives about interesting urban locations around the city delivered through mobile phones. The city-sponsored Live with Culture campaign, too, is a 16-month celebration of the extraordinary grassroots arts and cultural scene. On a broader economic note, the recently published Strategies for Creative Cities project brought together industry leaders to examine ways to lever the city's creative assets on to the global stage. Factor in other major annual events such as the Toronto International Film Festival – which has grown in attendance to become the world's largest film festival and will soon move into Festival Tower, with its own modern screening facility – and it is safe to say that creativity is indeed a way of life.

1   Meric Gertler. *Strategies for Creative Cities: Imagine a Toronto*,
     a report for the Strategies for Creative Cities Project, Toronto, 2006.
2   *Ibid.*
3   Daniel Libeskind, interview with the authors, Toronto, June 2006.

Art Gallery of Ontario

Gehry Partners

Dundas Street West, Toronto   2008

project
Art Gallery of Ontario
317 Dundas Street West, Toronto,
Ontario

architect
Gehry Partners, LLP

telephone
+1 416 979 6648

website
www.ago.net

opening hours
Mon–Tues: Closed
Wed–Fri: Noon to 9pm
Sat–Sun: 10am to 5:30pm

neighbourhood
nestled between Chinatown to the
west, funky Queen Street to the south,
and the charming restaurants of Baldwin
Street to the north

style
an unexpected combination of contorted
architectural bravura and refined modern
symmetry

clientele
students from the nearby Ontario
College of Art and Design mingle with
tourists and the creative curious

signature experience
standing behind the swooping transparent visor with uninterrupted views
to the street below

other projects
Guggenheim Museum, Bilbao; Pritzker
Pavilion, Millennium Park, Chicago; Walt
Disney Concert Hall, Los Angeles

What started as a simple conversation in early 2002, has led to an emotional and dramatic homecoming for internationally renowned architect Frank Gehry. When it was announced in 2004 that he would finally be designing his first major Canadian work in the city of his birth, the media frenzy was a spectacle in itself. Charged with the mandate to restore the connection between the Art Gallery of Ontario (AGO) and the city, and to clarify the internal layout, the project also raises some very interesting questions regarding expectations when a burgeoning *Design City* finally hires one of the world's most famous architects.

Known as Transformation AGO, the vision of the gallery was to transform the experience of art and increase its presence on the world stage. Not that the AGO needed the exposure; founded in 1900 by local citizens, the AGO has grown to become the tenth largest art museum in North America. The financial catalyst for the makeover is a CA$98 million donation from the late Canadian newspaper mogul Kenneth Thomson, and CA$48 million from Provincial SuperBuild funding. The remainder is expected to come from private donations and fundraising. Of the money donated by Thomson, CA$50 million in cash is earmarked for the expansion project, with the remainder consisting of over 2000 pieces of Canadian and European art from Thomson's private collection, including *Massacre of the Innocents* by Peter Paul Rubens.

The Art Gallery of Ontario is the first major Canadian commission for Gehry, although he is also working on a small winery in the Niagara wine region about one hour outside the city. The significance of the AGO project has not gone unnoticed, as it is literally steps from his childhood home. 'The Art Gallery of Ontario,' he said at the public unveiling, 'is where I first experienced art as a child and it was in Grange Park where I played.'

While the project bears few immediate resemblances to the signature billowing forms that have become his calling card, the design is certainly not wanting for architectural bravura. Stretching over 180 metres (590 feet) along the entire Dundas Street facade and rising 20 metres (65 feet) above street level will be a swooping Douglas fir and glass scrim that slants and twists over its full course and then breaks free from itself at the ends. Behind the transparent visor, a linear sculpture gallery will double as the main circulation route. On the south side of the gallery, a tinted glass and titanium tower will rise to overlook Grange Park and will house a hosting facility, galleries for contemporary art, and a panoramic dining hall. While a square box seems the last thing you would expect, a set of spiralling stairs bears the Gehry signature and twists its way through the skylit roof to the third and fourth floor contemporary galleries.

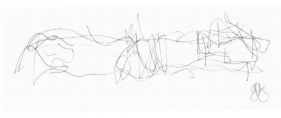

Left
An early conceptual sketch of the AGO
facade by Frank Gehry

Above
Even at the hands of Gehry, the AGO is
very much in the Toronto style; a somewhat modest contemporary building in
the heart of the city that respects the
scale of the neighbourhood in which it
resides

Right
Running an entire city block along
Dundas Avenue, the wood and glass
scrim bulges and twists before breaking
free from itself at either end

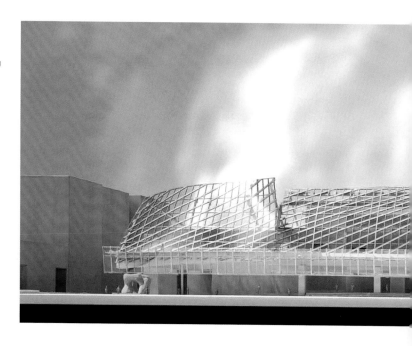

Below
Early schemes bore Gehry's signature
billowing foms

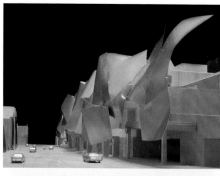

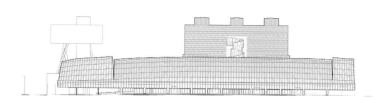

Above
The north elevation viewed from Dundas
Avenue *(above)* and the south elevation
viewed from Grange Park *(top)*

Left
Early ideas featuring graphics on the
glass scrim echo Graduate House by
Morphosis and Teeple Architects

Left
One early iteration featured a smooth
facade printed with a semi-transparent
frit of natural foliage

What is actually quite interesting is that the man best known for contorting the conventions of modern architecture has delivered a scheme that is an example of programmatic clarity. It is no secret to Torontonians that mazelike circulation was the gallery's Achilles heel. Gehry's response is a shift in the main entrance to restore the axial alignment with the classically arched Walker Court, the historic heart of the gallery. At the north-east corner, a social-gathering centre will engage the street through a bookshop, gift store, member's lounge, restaurant and a theatre.

Whether or not the AGO delivers the signature Gehry vernacular is debatable. Perhaps, however, its most laudable attribute is that it is very much in the Toronto style – a somewhat modest contemporary building in the heart of the city that respects the scale of the neighbourhood in which it resides. Yet, these good urban manners actually expose its most controversial aspect, its obvious comparison with the Guggenheim Museum in Bilbao, Spain, and the fundamental question it raises: are we to applaud Gehry's courage in departing from the object-building stereotype he has become synonymous with, or should we feel cheated out of our own 'Bilbao effect'? It is important to understand the pragmatic realities of the project. The city was reminded as early as 2002 that the AGO would not be similar to Bilbao as it simply did not have the physical space or the capital funding for such a grandiose gesture. But to believe that Toronto will be excluded from the global attention that comes with the Gehry brand is unrealistic as not all of his buildings are shimmering waves of titanium yet the international media still comes in droves.

While it is certainly not the iconic metallic sculpture that many expected, we can indeed rest assured that the AGO will be a truly wondrous experience of both art and architecture. And with so many other spectacular architectural works under way, including Daniel Libeskind's Crystal at the Royal Ontario Museum and the new Opera House by local architects Diamond + Schmitt, Toronto's Bilbao effect has already gained a momentum of its own.

Below
Behind the transparent visor, a linear sculpture gallery will double as the main circulation route overlooking Dundas Avenue

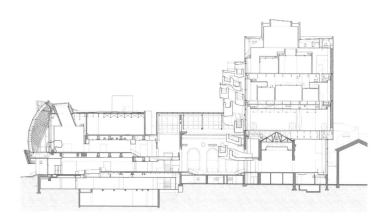

Left
North-south section through the sculpture gallery, Walker Court and the vertically stacked galleries for contemporary art

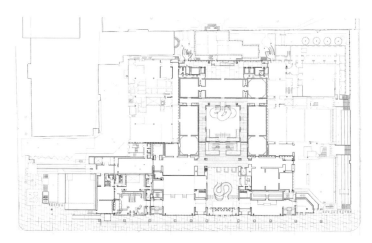

Left
Ground floor plan. The mazelike circulation was the gallery's Achilles heel. Gehry's plan restores programmatic clarity and axial alignment with the classically arched Walker Court – the historic heart of the gallery

Below
On the south side of the gallery a tinted glass and titanium tower will rise to overlook Grange Park

Right
A spiralling baroque stair bears the
Gehry signature and twists its way
through the skylit roof to the third and
fourth floor contemporary galleries

Right
In the main lobby and beyond, the fluid
lines synonymous with the Gehry style
take shape in the form of sweeping
stairs and ramps

Below
Schematic computer-generated models
of the full composition of new and existing buildings.

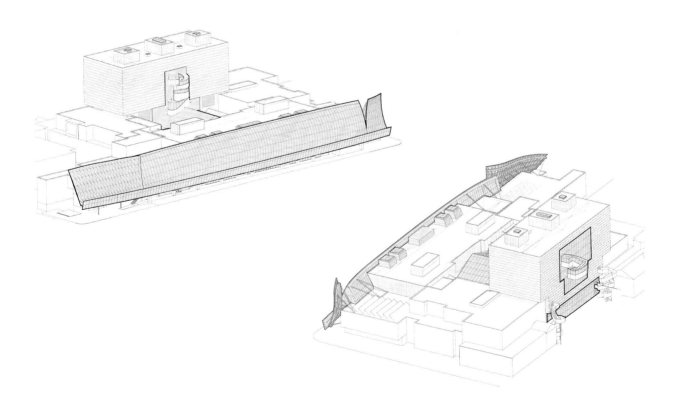

Bata Shoe Museum

Moriyama & Teshima Architects

Bloor Street West, Toronto   1995

project

Bata Shoe Museum
327 Bloor Street West, Toronto,
Ontario

architect
Moriyama & Teshima Architects

telephone
+1 416 979 7799

website
www.batashoemuseum.ca

opening hours
Tue–Wed + Fri–Sat: 10am to 5pm
Thurs: 10am to 8pm
Sun: Noon to 5pm

neighbourhood
in the museum district along Bloor
Street West, within walking distance
of the Royal Ontario Museum and
Gardiner Museum of Ceramic Art

style
a 'shoe-box' inspired container with
canted limestone walls and copper-
clad lid hovering over a ribbon of
display windows

clientele
shoe-o-holics and trendy Bloor Street
fashionistas

signature experience
standing across Bloor Street, watching the interplay of light and shadow
on the building's warm facade

other projects
Canadian War Museum, Ottawa;
Ryerson University Centre, Toronto;
The National Museum, Riyadh

In both architectural and curatorial circles, the Bata Shoe Museum is indeed a unique spectacle. Although its knife-cut styling and canted walls were precursors to the angular cubes of the Royal Ontario Museum expansion by Daniel Libeskind just a few blocks away, at the time of its opening, its deconstructivist form was unlike anything else in the city. On the inside, the museum houses one of the most remarkable collections of footwear in the world, spanning 4500 years of history with over 10,000 items from every geographical corner of the world.

The owner, Sonja Bata (Chair of the Bata Shoe Museum Foundation who also studied architecture in her native Switzerland), has been personally amassing shoes since the 1940s, and the collection – which includes every kind of footwear imaginable – is indeed spectacular. From plush red velvet slippers embroidered with gold cruciforms worn by Pope Pius VII to the single running shoe worn by national hero Terry Fox during his Marathon of Hope, each boot, sandal and slipper has a unique history and evocative story to be told.

With such a broad palette of history, narrative and materials to work from, the mandate put to architect Raymond Moriyama was quite simple – to create a 'small gem of a museum'. The result, apparent to most observers, is a modest three-storey building set to the proportions of a shoe box with its lid slightly ajar. While modest in size, this is no ordinary shoe box. From the outside, the most prominent feature is the two street-facing walls. Canted inward at an angle of 83.2 degrees, to provide greater space along the pavement, the walls are clad in an exceptional French ochre limestone. With the soft sheen, warm luminosity and fine texture of raw leather – a basic material of the shoe industry – the walls respond with a cadence that taps into nature's rhythm of light and shadow. On sunny days, reflections from across the street sweep across the tilted planes, while the late afternoon sun casts a rich golden glow that slowly transforms into a soft magenta with the setting sun. Overhead, the shadow-dance is furthered by the large copper roof that sits slightly askew, resembling a lid resting on an open box protecting its contents from harmful ultraviolet rays of the sun. And when nature cannot deliver the desired candle-power, a variety of artificial light sources in the soffit and in the pavement flood the wall face.

Located at the busy corner of Bloor and St George Streets, the museum occupies a convenient midtown location directly across from the subway station and within walking distance of the Royal Ontario Museum, Gardiner Museum of Ceramic Art, and University of Toronto. To tap into this daily flow of people, and to reward the curious, the entire stone mass

Opposite
A simple maple and glass staircase rises through the main atrium, providing contrast to surrounding vibrant displays

Above
With some 65,000 visitors passing
through its doors annually, the Bata Shoe
Museum is part of a wonderful journey of
discovery and new awareness

Below
A glimpse at the restoration of some of
the museum's delicate artefacts

discover
Explore

Above
The small gem of a museum is housed
in a modest three-storey building set to
the proportions of a shoe box with its
lid slightly ajar

hovers above the pavement via a band of glazed display cases, while a two-storey glass prism pierces the limestone mass and protrudes directly into the pedestrian's path. Equally drawing attention to the entry, a warped copper strut shoots through the walls and thankfully stabilises the seemingly dangerous canted walls.

The location of the entry, the precise angle of the canted walls and the exact position of the cantilevered roof are by no means random. Moriyama is a master in manipulating light to create dramatic visual spectacles, so both by way of luck in site selection, and intentionally by design, the angled shadows cast by the roof align precisely with the entry wedge and meet exactly at its apex.

Through the wedge, you can see directly into the heart of the building; a light-filled volume containing the central hall and lobby, a cantilevered steel and glass staircase, and a dramatic 13-metre-high (42 feet) art-glass/sculptural installation created by artist Lutz Haufschild. A collage of painted, fired, clear and bevelled glass sections, the window casts colourful rainbows and refracted silhouettes across the walls and floors. Drawing attention downward as visitors move through the building, the designers intentionally incorporated a number of foot-inspired details including glass balustrades, see-through gaps in the stairs and patterns of diagonals and wedges in the highly reflective white stone flooring.

Set behind the exterior limestone planes are the major exhibition galleries, gift shop, multipurpose rooms, special display spaces and administrative functions, with additional galleries located on two levels below ground. In keeping with the original seed of the museum as a neutral container, the galleries are simple and largely unadorned with special design features. In this way, curators and exhibit designers are free to create displays unique to the delicate objects being viewed. Interestingly, a subtle homage to the history of shoemaking and the cobbler's skills is provided through cast bronze and leather signage – a detail probably noticed only by devout shoe-o-holics.

In as much as you would never wear sneakers to a gala evening at the opera, Moriyama has created a wonderfully appropriate sculptural response that acts as a transition from the fast-paced Bloor Street through to the exhibit spaces and the frail objects on display. With some 65,000 visitors passing through its doors annually, the Bata Shoe Museum has become a popular venue for private functions and, much to the delight of its owner, is part of a wonderful journey of discovery and new awareness.

Opposite
The museum houses one of the most
remarkable collections of footwear in
the world, spanning 4500 years of
history with over 10,000 items from
every geographical corner of the world

Above
A collage of painted, fired, clear, and bevelled glass sections by artist Lutz Haufschild casts colourful rainbows and refracted silhouettes across the walls and floors

Right
The angle of the canted walls and the exact position of the entry tap into the flow of traffic on Bloor Street and direct visitors into the main lobby

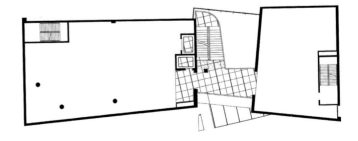

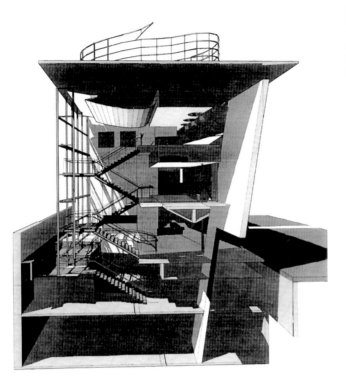

Left
The heart of the building is a light-filled central hall and lobby featuring a canti-levered steel and glass staircase, and a dramatic 13-metre-high (42 feet) art-glass installation

Below
The angled shadows cast by the roof align precisely with the entry wedge and meet exactly at its apex

Bata Shoe Museum

Evergreen Commons at The Brick Works

Evergreen / John van Nostrand / architectsAlliance

Don River Valley, Toronto   2006

With the international spotlight now brightly illuminating the city's archi-cultural renaissance, it is important to remember that being a true *Design City* means more than just having a collection of flamboyant iconic works by internationally-renowned architects. In fact, it is a holistic state of stewardship that resides at the convergence of quality urban spaces, contemporary architecture, heritage preservation and green initiatives. With this in mind, leading the charge is an environmental group known as Evergreen with their project at the Toronto Brick Works. A unique natural and physical rejuvenation project, Evergreen Commons will celebrate, in one location, the peaceful coexistence of seemingly polar opposite conditions: our natural ravine and wetland systems and the city's once rich and vibrant industrial legacy.

Nestled deep in the heart of the Don River valley, the Toronto Brick Works is one of the city's last remaining industrial denizens from the late 1800s. Originally founded by the Taylor family, the factory churned out during its heyday over 43 million bricks a year, most of which were used to create many of the city's still prominent landmarks including Old City Hall, Casa Loma, and Massey Hall. With the last kiln firing in 1984, the 43-acre brownfield site was abandoned and its factories fell victim to gradual neglect and continual vandalism.

Purchased by the Toronto Region Conservation Authority (TRCA) in 1985, the site today consists of several derelict industrial sheds and a system of regenerated natural wetlands that feed into the Lower Don watershed. Despite being designated a heritage property, the buildings themselves are not that architecturally significant, beyond their obvious photogenic qualities for industrial archaeologists. However, the exterior of the utilitarian sheds bears little evidence of the luminous drama that waits within. For those willing to ignore the 'No Trespassing' signs and secretly venture over the chain link fence, there are just rewards. Inside, rows of massive brick kilns and heavy pressing machinery sit under a dusting of red clay powder, while metal catwalks and decaying ductwork shoot through with an eerie calm. As focused beams of light and drops of rain stream through holes in the rusted tin roof, you can't help imagining the long-silenced sounds of industry in the background.

For all its photographic drama, the real value to the city is not in its architecture but in its ecology. Toronto is blessed with a vast network of natural ravines and watersheds unlike any other in North America. In fact the ravine system is as unique to Toronto as the canals are to Venice or the hills are to San Francisco. The backlands and the quarry too have been recognised internationally for the Pleistocene geology, Carolinian forests, and fossil deposits that are over 300,000 years old. As part of its

project
Evergreen Commons at The Brick Works
550 Bayview Avenue, Toronto, Ontario

architect
Evergreen / John van Nostrand / architectsAlliance

telephone
+1 416 596 1495

website
www.evergreen.ca/en/brickworks

opening hours
not yet available

neighbourhood
in the floodplain of the Don River, a designated heritage site of historic industrial buildings surrounded by hiking trails, meadows, and gardens

style
a Gaudí-esque collage, the masterplan weaves three themes of nature, culture and community along a series of inter-connected nature trails

clientele
a mix of nature lovers, foodies, students and local artisans

signature experience
eating a meal made from fresh produce grown on-site in the demonstration gardens

other projects
Evergreen: Toyota Evergreen Learning Grounds, Nationwide; Evergreen Lawn and Garden Smart, Vancouver
architectsAlliance: St George Street Revitalisation, Toronto; York University Computer Science Building, Toronto

Opposite
The site is a precarious maze of obstacles and broken relics of industrial machinery

broader initiative for natural preservation, the TRCA has been undertaking an aggressive regeneration process of the valley's brownlands since 1995. But even with the support of the TRCA and the city, what the Brick Works really needed was a holistic and environmentally viable development scheme. Enter Evergreen.

Guided by their mission, The Nature of Cities, Evergreen is a national non-profit organisation dedicated to the promotion of environmental stewardship and the recognition of nature's place in our cities. With executive director Geoff Cape at the helm, Evergreen has set in motion a bold initiative that will transform this deteriorating brownfield relic into a mixed-use, environmentally conscious cultural asset. Under the three themes of nature, culture and community, the Brick Works will become a year-round centre for experiential learning and offer education on how nature can make cities more liveable. Acting as a natural gateway to the city's extensive network of ravines, wetlands and walking trails, the site and its future interpretive discovery centre will host upwards of 250,000 visitors a year, showcasing all things green from woodworking and gardening classes, to YMCA summer camp activities and a slow-food café run by celebrated restaurateur Jamie Kennedy.

At the heart of the project will be Evergreen Gardens, a 10,000-square-metre (12,000 squre yards) demonstration garden and native plant nursery. In order to fully experience the site, a network of pathways will snake their way around to connect the buildings with the existing ravine system. To be finished in a Gaudí-esque collage of materials and found *objets d'art*, the pathways will be perfect for walking in the summer and, where possible, will be flooded to form natural skating rinks in the winter. Other activities in the works include an outdoor performance space, a small television studio for taping gardening and cooking segments, and an

Below
Founded by the Taylor family, the Brick Works churned out over 43 million bricks a year during its heyday, most of which were used to create many of the city's still prominent landmarks

Above
The city's ravine system is as unique to Toronto as hills are to San Francisco. Today, the backlands and the quarry have been recognised internationally for the Pleistocene geology, Carolinian forests, and fossil deposits that are over 300,000 years old

Left
Acting as a natural gateway to the city's network of ravines and wetlands, the Brick Works will host upwards of 250,000 visitors a year showcasing all things green

artisan market featuring the Brick Works wood shop, to be run in partnership with the YMCA and its at-risk youth programme.

The masterplan, completed by local architect and urban planner John van Nostrand (architectsAlliance), has been endorsed by virtually everyone from private donors to City Council and the Mayor's office. A significant gift of CA$3 million was pledged by founding patrons Robin and David Young and Family. The project has even raised eyebrows at Federal level as the Ministry of Culture recently pledged CA$10 million in project support and in fact it was the only heritage preservation initiative to be identified in the annual national budget speech.

With architecture and urban design now a key piece in the city's cultural and civic agenda, it really is no surprise that Evergreen's concept is receiving such a warm welcome and is well on its way to becoming a reality. Beyond furthering a sustainable urban mandate, the city already has the necessary elements in place: an extensive network of verdant ravines, a growing collective mindset towards environmental awareness, and a new-found appreciation for preserving heritage sites, despite a track record of being unkind to heritage buildings during the 1970s. While the Brick Works is not the first restoration of its kind in the city, as evidenced by the recent restoration of the Gooderham and Worts Distillery District or the Gladstone Hotel, what makes Evergreen's plan unique is that the entire site eschews commercialisation in favour of becoming a self-sustaining, eco-tourism resource.

Below
A maze of decaying ducts, which once exhausted hot air from the kilns, shoots overhead within the rafters

Above
With our new-found appreciation for preserving heritage sites in a more sustainable manner, the heart of the project will be Evergreen Gardens, a 10,000-square-metre (12,000 square yards) demonstration garden and native plant nursery

Right
Once the original brick kilns are removed, the kiln shed will be converted into the farmers' market and a slow-food café

Right
Rows of massive brick kilns sit silent while metal catwalks and decaying ductwork are suspended overhead

discover
Explore

Left
The restored kiln shed will feature an organic farmers' market and 'slow-food' café run by celebrated restaurateur Jamie Kennedy

Left
In the summer, the paths will be perfect for walking and, where possible, will be flooded to form natural skating rinks in the winter

Left
What the Brick Works really needed was a holistic and environmentally viable development scheme. Enter Evergreen

Right
Decorated with a Gaudí-esque collage of materials and found objets d'art, a network of pathways will snake their way through the 43-acre brownfield site

discover
Explore

The new Evergreen Commons will
celebrate, in one location, the peaceful
coexistence of seemingly polar opposite
conditions: our natural ravine and wetland systems and the city's once rich
and vibrant industrial legacy

Evergreen Commons at The Brick Works

Kuwabara Payne McKenna Blumberg Architects

King Street West, Toronto   2009

project

Toronto International Film Festival, Festival Centre and Tower
Corner of King Street West and John Street, Toronto, Ontario

architect

Kuwabara Payne McKenna Blumberg Architects, with the Toronto International Film Festival Group

telephone

+1 416 967 7371

website

www.festivalcentre.ca

opening hours

to be completed 2009

neighbourhood

at the heart of the Entertainment District, Toronto's premiere entertainment destination for theatres, restaurants, shops and nightspots

style

a transparent modern glass podium topped by a residential condominium

clientele

film lovers, media mavens and cultural tourists

signature experience

watching a movie under the stars from the rooftop outdoor amphitheatre

other projects

Japanese Canadian Cultural Centre, Toronto; Canadian Embassy, Berlin

Starting in 1976 as an independent film event featuring a montage of the best films from other international festivals, the Toronto International Film Festival (TIFF) has grown by attendance to become the world's largest film festival and is widely considered, after Cannes, to be the premier cinematic event from which the Oscar race begins. Beginning the first Thursday after Labour Day (first Monday in September in Canada), the festival lasts for 10 days during which around 400 films are screened at approximately 23 venues across the city.

The cultural and economic impact of the festival on the city is immense – generating almost CA\$67 million, including CA\$33 million in tourist dollars. But while playing host to Hollywood's A-listers, swarms of tourists and the usual horde of international media, as well as coordinating a variety of related cinematic programmes and sub-festivals during the year including a children's film festival, it seems inconceivable that the festival organisation could actually be 'homeless'. Divided between 200 separate external venues across the city, it became evident that the Festival Group not only desperately needed a singular venue to host the festival, but also desired a unique showcase for Canadian and international filmmakers and, of course, a place for the media-mavens to simply celebrate all-things film.

Due to be completed in 2009, Festival Centre and Tower is poised to become Toronto's cinematic nexus. Dispersed within a five-floor podium of 14,000 square metres (16,750 square yards), the Centre will include four dedicated theatres and one swing theatre offering 1300 cinema seats; a film resource library for over 14,000 volumes; a gallery to display rare memorabilia collections by notable Canadians David Cronenberg and Atom Egoyan; and multiple learning centres offering student courses, public screenings, workshops, and industry seminars. The Centre will also provide a creative workplace for staff and volunteers of the Festival Group's highly successful programmes including Sprockets, Talk Cinema and Cinematheque Ontario. In addition to the bar, restaurant and café on the lower level podium, there will also be a romantic outdoor, rooftop amphitheatre to screen films under the stars. To the north, a 37-storey tower will contain private residential suites.

Part of the challenge also came in the form of finding a suitable site. Thanks to the generosity of the King and John Festival Corporation – a joint venture between Canadian producer and director Ivan Reitman, his sisters Susan Michaels and Agi Mandel, and the Daniels Corporation who are selling the land at King and John Streets well below market value – the Festival Centre will sit right at the heart of the John Street media corridor. Alongside many of the city's prominent media venues, the site is within easy walking distance of the headquarters for the National Film Board, the Canadian Broadcasting Corporation (designed by Philip Johnson), the CN Tower and the Rogers Centre (formerly the SkyDome), and of course

nd Tower

Above

The theatres will be expressed by raked dark zinc cubes that project through the facade. An added layer of dimension will be created through a horizontal montage of clear, fritted and translucent glass bands that will provide silhouettes and still frames of the action within

the Theatre District where the Princess of Wales Theatre, the Royal Alexandra Theatre and the Roy Thomson Hall can be found among a smart strip of restaurants, cafés and hotels.

Architecturally, the design of Festival Centre is very much in keeping with the filmic aspects of transparency and luminosity and is decidedly a Kuwabara Payne McKenna Blumberg building in its expression. The podium is designed and proportioned to mimic the typical twentieth-century loft buildings prevalent in the area. The theatres will be expressed by raked dark zinc-clad cubes that project through the podium's facade and are highlighted by illuminated vertical panels of

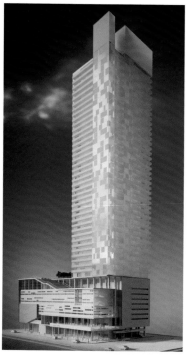

Above
Festival Centre and Tower will become Toronto's cinematic nexus. Dispersed within a five floor podium will be four dedicated theatres and one swing theatre offering 1,300 cinema seats. Above, the tower will contain private residential suites

Left
Finished with stone floors, warm wood and frosted glass, the theatre lobby will be animated by media screens, electronic billboards, and colourful banners

discover
Explore

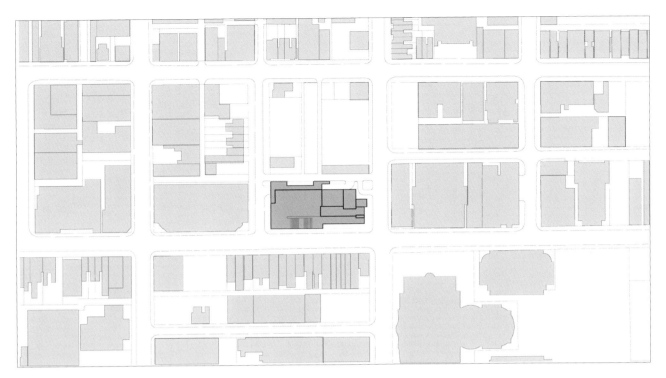

frosted glass. An added dimension will be created through a horizontal montage of clear, fritted and translucent glass bands that will provide silhouettes and snapshots of the action within.

At street level, an extended concrete canopy will lead visitors directly to the box office. Highlighted by integrated linear lighting, the effect on the pavement will intensify the red-carpet experience. The tower element will assume a very different language and will take its expressional cues from the city's modernist towers of the 1950s and '60s. Wrapped in limestone and a mosaic of aluminium and glass panels, from clear to frosted for varying degrees of transparency, the contemporary figure will blend in with the silhouette of the city skyline. Suites in the tower will range from 40 square metres (48 square yards) to a sumptuous 370-square-metre (440 square yards) penthouse. Residents will also have unique access to the film collection and special film-related events and programmes.

Once inside the double-height entry hall, the cityscape will serve as a backdrop for gala events. Finished with warm limestone and retro-plated concrete, the space will be further animated by media screens, electronic billboards, and colourful banners. The two-storey bar and restaurant on the corner of King and John Streets will be connected to the Centre on both levels providing exciting networking opportunities. On the second floor, the screening rooms will be expressed as individual blocks and clad in panels of Douglas fir, while the library and resource centre will occupy a significant part of the fourth floor. The most exciting aspect of the design will undoubtedly be the outdoor amphitheatre, with the raked concrete seating inspired by the stepped roof of the Villa Malaparte on the Isle of Capri, a classic icon of film and architecture.

To realise this vision, the Festival Group is mounting a comprehensive campaign aimed at raising CA$196 million, of which CA$132 million has already been collected at the time of writing. The commitment of the various levels of government, in combination with the generosity of private corporations and individuals, are certainly key factors in making the dream of Festival Centre a reality. If all the stars continue to align, the Festival Centre and Tower will break ground by 2007 and will inspire audiences of all ages by offering a dynamic, entertaining and transformative experience, just like a night at the movies.

Right
Early conceptual sketch of the podium base and the main entry

Right
The plan is arranged around the central atrium. Once inside, the atrium will provide a place for meeting, gathering and orientation for special events

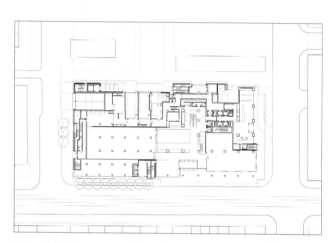

Below
At street level, an extended concrete canopy will wrap the corner and lead visitors directly to the box office. Highlighted by integrated linear lighting, the effect on the pavement will intensify the red-carpet experience

discover
Explore

Right
The movement of people up to the
second- and third-floor lobbies will be
via a combination of escalators, stairs
and bridges, creating an urban interior
experience

Right
By day the glass facade blends into
the space of the street, while at night
the illuminated cube glows like a jewel

Seasons Centre
for the Perfoming Arts

Diamond + Schmitt Architects Inc
Queen Street West, Toronto   2006

It was born as a grand civic project that started back in the well-heeled early 1980s. Now, after patiently waiting nearly 20 years and having been teased with countless design schemes and as many elected governments, the city of Toronto finally has its opera house. And while it may not be a high-profile landmark like those of Sydney or Los Angeles, ours is a democratic citadel preaching good urban manners that welcomes and opens its doors to anyone who comes. Refusing to make a spectacle of itself, when it could easily do so, it is downright humble about its modernist attributes; in short, it is about as Toronto as it gets.

Designed by local architectural impresario Jack Diamond of Diamond + Schmitt Architects Inc, the Four Seasons Centre for the Performing Arts replaces the existing Hummingbird (formerly O'Keefe) Centre, as the new home for the Canadian Opera Company (COC) and the National Ballet of Canada. At nearly 37,000 square metres (44,250 square yards), the hall is actually Canada's first purpose-built opera house.

Architecturally, purpose-built is exactly what it is, as Diamond has intentionally chosen to put function before glamour. The building occupies a prominent corner block at University Avenue and Queen Street, both significant urban arteries in their own right, and is one of the few buildings in the city to lay claim to four full street frontages. The exterior, however, is kept intentionally modest; in fact, you could miss it entirely when travelling at speed along University Avenue. Exuding a slightly modernist-industrial feel, the building is essentially composed from three fairly conventional building blocks – a single mass of dark-charcoal brick that contains the performance hall and working stages, and two fully-transparent glass cubes clipped on to the north and west sides of the shiny brick edifice. By day the glass facade blends into the space of the street, while at night the illuminated cube glows like a jewel. With its clean lines and plenty of glass, the opera house is a perfect example of the refined modernism that has now become synonymous with the Toronto style.

The building opts to politely blend into the city fabric instead of standing out, which comes as no surprise as Diamond – and his then partner Barton Myers – began promoting an adaptive modernist style in the early 1970s. But unlike other significant cultural projects in the city that compete for street presence through their blatant exhibitionism, Diamond loathes trophy architecture and iconic spectacles that bulge and contort simply for the sake of it, and in fact considers it anti-urban. In a recent summit sponsored by the American Institute of Architects on the subject of Toronto's renaissance, Diamond gestured, 'In Canada, individualism of extremes is not always favoured. It's easy to do the spectacular, grand

project
Four Seasons Centre for the Performing Arts
145 Queen Street West, Toronto, Ontario

architect
Diamond + Schmitt Architects Inc

telephone
+1 416 363 6671

website
www.fourseasonscentre.ca

opening hours
not available

neighbourhood
where commerce meets the arts: east of the funky Queen Street arts district and close to the downtown business core

style
a perfect example of the refined glass modernism that has become synonymous with the Toronto style

clientele
Toronto's cultural elite and the musically curious who come to enjoy an opera or free daytime performance

signature experience
sitting 2.5 metres from the stage in an orchestra ring seat, with full view of the conductor leading the performance of Wagner's Ring Cycle

other projects
Richmond Hill Central Library, Richmond Hill; York University Student Centre, Toronto

Left
With its modest disposition, the opera house is a democratic citadel preaching good urban manners that opens its doors to anyone who comes. In short, it is about as Toronto as it gets

gesture, but how do you create something more than ordinary – give it importance – and still fit the city? [1]

While Diamond remains unapologetic about the building's lack of flamboyance, and while he may have eschewed the drama that is often associated with an operatic performance, the building is not without its exuberance. Nowhere is this better expressed than in the aptly named City Room, a five-storey skylit loft that is actually a combination of entrance lobby and performance space. Inside what is essentially a giant fishbowl, an oversized staircase hovers unsupported overhead. Clad in a honey-coloured maple, the stepped slab doubles as an interior amphitheatre where guests can sit on loose cushions to hear free concerts, recitals or lectures. Clipped on to the inside edge of the oversized slab is a whimsical frosted glass staircase. Lit from within by halogen spotlights, the glass stair adds a layer of sparkle to the room. On the opposite interior wall, a beechwood latticed screen bulges and arches to mimic the performance hall while back-lit silhouettes of opera-goers filter through from behind.

Essential to the culture of opera is the elitist notion of seeing and being seen. Offering panoramic views both in and out, the City Room recruits University Avenue and the city itself as its perpetual live backdrop, while at the same time, the audience inadvertently becomes theatrical divas for passers-by on the pavement below – a very democratic experience indeed. In music, the rests between the notes are as important as the notes themselves in that they accentuate the experience yet to come. In contrast to the vibrant City Room, the equally glazed Donor Room on the north face is noticeably perfectly quiet and offers a brief pause between city and opera. Sitting on the full-length wooden bench overlooking busy Queen Street, with the din of the streetcars silenced, is reminiscent of that very brief moment when the music and the city stops, if only for a second.

Nestled like an egg in its nest, the performance hall is an experience unto itself as the crisp lines of the City Room give way to sensual curves and soft colours. Designed in the traditional horseshoe shape like its classic counterparts La Scala in Milan or the Garnier in Paris, the hall offers near perfect acoustics. Again in the spirit of seeing and being seen, the horseshoe allows the audience to have a view of each other as well as the

discover
Explore

Above
In contrast to the vibrant City Room, the equally glazed Donor Room on the north face is perfectly silent and offers a brief pause between city and opera

Right
In the City Room, an oversized staircase clad in a honey-coloured maple doubles as an interior amphitheatre where guests can sit on loose cushions to hear free concerts, recitals or lectures

Right

With seating for nearly 2000, the hall
feels much more intimate and smaller
than it really is; in fact, 73 per cent of
the audience is within 30 metres (98
feet) of the stage, a major achievement
on such a tight site

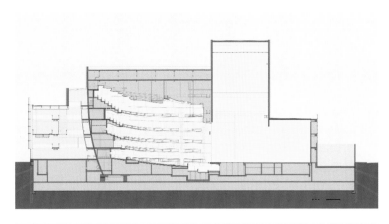

Right

The building is essentially composed of
three fairly conventional building blocks.
Working from the performance hall outward, the hall is nestled like an egg in
its nest

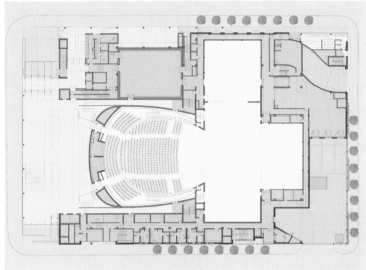

Below

A whimsical frosted glass staircase
floats overhead. Lit from within by
halogen spotlights, the glass stair
adds a layer of sparkle to the room

stage. No right angles are to be found here. Clad in a tan-coloured beech,
four tiers of seating gradually ramp their way upward, while the undulating
walls are textured to emulate the finest suede and are tinted a subtle blend
somewhere between mushroom and elephant. Overhead, the rounded
convex ceiling emulates the fluid pattern of the balconies, but also adds a
cosmological touch by mimicking the rings of Saturn. With seating for
nearly 2,000, the hall feels much more intimate and smaller than it really
is; in fact, 73 per cent of the audience is within 30 metres (98 feet) of the
stage, which is quite an achievement for such a tight urban site. Naturally,
acoustics were a prime concern, particularly when the hall sits directly
over the subway. To resolve this, the entire hall is physically separated
from the rest of the building and literally floats on 500 rubber pads set
deep in the foundations.

What the Four Seasons Centre for the Performing Arts does best
though, is acknowledge that opera is no longer the pastime of the urban
elite and, as such, makes itself welcome to everyone. It may not have the
recognisable sail-like forms of Sydney, or the rich history of Europe's
classic halls, but it is uniquely Torontonian in its modernist styling. And
while it may be shy about its place in the city, it still offers plenty of the
flamboyant attributes that come with a night at the opera.

1   Kristen Richards. *Starchitecture and the City: Toronto's Bilbao Effect?*,
     eOculus, 17 October 2005 – *www.aiany.org/eOCULUS/2005*

Right
Four tiers of seating gradually ramp their way upward, while the undulating walls are textured to emulate the finest suede and are tinted a subtle blend somewhere between mushroom and elephant

Below
New home to the Canadian Opera Company and the National Ballet of Canada, the 37,000-square-metre (44,250 square yards) hall is Canada's first purpose-built opera house

Four Seasons Centre for Performing Arts

Gardiner Museum
of Ceramic Art

Kuwabara Payne McKenna Blumberg Architects

Queen's Park Circle, Toronto   2006

project
Gardiner Museum of Ceramic Art
111 Queen's Park Circle, Toronto, Ontario

architect
Kuwabara Payne McKenna Blumberg Architects

telephone
+1 416 586 8080

website
www.gardinermuseum.on.ca

opening hours
Mon – Thurs, Sat – Sun: 10am to 6pm
Fri: 10am to 9pm
Library
Mon: 1pm to 4pm by appointment

neighbourhood
in the exclusive Bloor Street area, near the major designer stores, museums, and prestige hotels

style
a series of buff-coloured limestone and glass 'jewel-boxes' stack themselves up and out over the urban forecourt

clientele
professional potters, ceramic enthusiasts and student artists-in-the-making

signature experience
pounding, rolling, and sculpting your own personal work of art in one of the museum's clay classes

other projects
Canadian Museum of Nature, Ottawa; Goodman Theatre, Chicago

The crossroads of University Avenue and Bloor Street is one of Toronto's premier cultural intersections. Most of the credit, of course, can be attributed to the expansion of the Royal Ontario Museum (ROM) and its outrageously bold Libeskind Crystal, complemented by the high-end retail and private galleries of Yorkville just one block north. However, sitting modestly across from the ROM is a small and intimate gallery which, throughout its 20-year tenure, has emerged as one of the city's outstanding cultural institutions. Dedicated entirely to the research, interpretation and display of ceramic art, the Gardiner Museum of Ceramic Art is a unique gem in the city's architectural and cultural renaissance.

Open since 1984, the Gardiner is one of the city's few private niche galleries that cater to a specific audience, a title it shares with the Textile Museum and the Bata Shoe Museum. The brainchild of philanthropists George and Helen Gardiner, the gallery was conceived as a vehicle to share their outstanding private ceramics collection with the city. The Gardiners first began collecting in the late 1970s; today the museum contains more than 2,900 pieces including the world's most impressive cache of European pottery and porcelain from the fifteenth to the nineteenth centuries. Before his death, George Gardiner – a successful financier and former chairman of the Toronto Stock Exchange – donated a CA$15 million endowment to the museum, thereby ensuring its longevity, while as Chair of the George and Helen Gardiner Charitable Foundation, Helen remains active in the Toronto arts community. With additional funding from private sector donors, the Provincial and Federal governments, and a newly-formed partnership with Jamie Kennedy, one of Canada's most lauded chefs, the Gardiner now delivers a world-class cultural experience on a par with its big brother across the street.

A popular expression suggests that 'diamonds are created under pressure'. In the case of the Gardiner, this pressure was a good thing; in the past five years its collection has grown exponentially, membership has more than doubled and its educational programmes have also experienced fantastic growth attracting more than 14,000 schoolchildren each year. To meet these new demands, the museum launched its All Fired Up! building initiative and hired architects Kuwabara Payne McKenna Blumberg to completely renovate and expand the original building. Led by Bruce Kuwabara, Shirley Blumberg and Paolo Rocha, the architects added over 900 square metres (1075 square yards) of new space. With an enhanced education centre, a glazed entry atrium, three new galleries for contemporary ceramics, and a terraced forecourt, the museum makes strong cultural and academic connections with the city it was always meant to serve.

Beyond being unable to adequately display its extensive collection, the Achilles heel of the original museum really was a lack of 'kerb' appeal and its poor relationship with the street. Once a humble charcoal-coloured

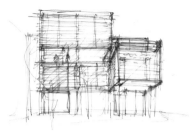

Left
Early conceptual sketch of the main entrance facade

Above
The museum contains more than 2900 pieces, including the world's most impressive cache of European pottery and porcelain from the fifteenth to the nineteenth centuries

Right
No longer dark and uninviting, the gallery engages the visitor in a wonderfully choreographed experience moving through the landscaped forecourt and across a small entry bridge

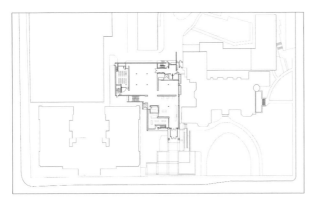

Left
The elegant plan adds 900 square
metres (1075 square yards) of new
space, including a glazed entry atrium,
three new galleries for contemporary
ceramics, and a terraced forecourt

Right
Set back from the street on a raised plinth of offset stairs and ramps, a series of buff-coloured limestone and glass 'jewel-boxes' stack themselves up and out to provide three floors of much needed display space

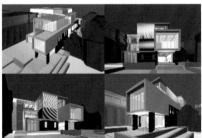

Above
The museum sits confidently between the neoclassical Lillian Massey Building to the north and the American Queen Anne-style Margaret Addison Hall to the south (top) where, as the early renderings (above) show, the many facades of glass act as lenses that grant uninterrupted views deep inside the galleries

Left
Dedicated entirely to the exhibition, research and interpretation of ceramic art, the Gardiner Museum of Ceramic Art has slowly emerged as one of the city's outstanding cultural institutions

box that went largely unnoticed from the pavement, the museum now presides over its site with confidence and prowess. Set back from the street on a raised plinth of offset stairs and ramps, a series of buff-coloured limestone and glass 'jewel-boxes' stack themselves up and out to provide three floors of much needed display space. When viewed from the pavement, the intimate scale and soft hues of the limestone provide an elegant transition between the neoclassical Lillian Massey Building to the north (now the Club Monaco flagship store) and the American Queen Anne-style Margaret Addison Hall to the south. By day, the limestone blocks project a sense of permanence and confidence, while at night the facade dissolves behind a series of horizontal louvres permitting an elegant filigree of night light to flood the plaza.

The new galleries are open and full of light and engage the visitor in a series of wonderfully choreographed experiences. As you approach through the landscaped forecourt and across a small entry bridge, the many facades of glass act as lenses that grant uninterrupted views deep inside the galleries and the shop. Inside, the journey through the collection continues across a series of platforms and changing levels, with unexpected vistas and small intimate moments. Throughout the various rooms, the finishes vary depending on the level and function and include buff-grey limestone, dark carpeting, black terrazzo and bleached white oak.

On the ground and second floors, the spaces have been reconfigured to house two additional collections, Asian porcelains and the new contemporary ceramics, and also a new specialty retail space. The expanded Education Centre will give students and seniors greater access to the award-winning hands-on clay programmes, while the new Curatorial Research Centre will play home to the largest ceramics library in Canada. Additionally, the Gardiner will now, for the first time, be able to host international touring exhibitions, further increasing the gallery's international cachet. Of course, the vertical ascent culminates in the new Jamie Kennedy restaurant (modelled after the already successful Jamie Kennedy Wine Bar also featured in this book) and outdoor rooftop terraces with never-before-seen panoramas of the city skyline.

Architecturally, the solution is quite elegant, proving that bigger isn't always better when it comes to asserting an urban presence. Celebrating small and intimate moments that inform and educate – much like the pieces on display – the Gardiner is a very mature addition to an already prominent urban boulevard and as such it achieves its ultimate goal: to reconnect the museum with its *Design City*.

Left
A series of horizontal louvres adorn the front facade

Below
The new galleries are open and full of light, engaging the visitor in a series of choreographed experiences as they move about

Above
Spectacular views and tapas-style dining can be enjoyed at Jamie Kennedy at the Gardiner, operated by one of Canada's most lauded chefs

Left
Included in the renovation and expansion of the original building are an enhanced education centre, a new glazed entry atrium, a shop, and three new galleries for contemporary ceramics

Left
Educational programmes at the Gardiner attract more than 14,000 schoolchildren each year

Young Centre for Performing Arts

Kuwabara Payne McKenna Blumberg Architects

Mill Street, Toronto   2006

project

Young Centre for Performing Arts

55 Mill Street, Building 49, Toronto, Ontario

architect

Kuwabara Payne McKenna Blumberg Architects

telephone

+1 416 866 8666

website

www.soulpepper.ca

opening hours

Tues – Sat: box office open 1pm to 8pm

neighbourhood

in the historic Distillery District, the largest single concentration of industrial Victorian buildings in North America

style

Warehouse refined – rough walls envelop cosy theatre spaces

clientele

theatre, dance and music aficionados

signature experience

enjoying the warmth of the central fireplace, watching theatregoers stroll along the cobblestone streets outside

other projects

Kitchener City Hall, Kitchene, Ontario; Le Quartier Concordia, Montreal

Toronto is very fortunate in that there is a fairly large stock of intact historical buildings, many of which are finding new life as key pieces in the city's architectural renaissance. When supported by patrons of the arts who are willing to donate large sums to ensure their longevity and reuse, the result is often a wonderfully restored civic building that benefits both the city as a whole, and the local arts community it serves.

The Young Centre for Performing Arts is just such a venue. The progeny of a special partnership between George Brown College and the Soulpepper Theatre Company, the hybrid theatre challenges the prototypical models for small theatres by integrating teaching and live performance spaces with training and youth outreach opportunities, all set within the backdrop of the restored nineteenth-century Gooderham & Worts Distillery District.

Occupying the simple, red-brick Tank Houses numbers 9 and 10 and the newly-enclosed spaces between them, theatre-goers and performers are treated to a unique ensemble of time, architectural history, culture and performance. To pass through the iron gates of the original distillery is to be transported back in time to a Dickensian world of narrow cobblestone streets and Victorian brick buildings replete with the still odorous relics of a long forgotten era. In fact, many of these original remnants still dot the 13-acre site. Antique steel hoppers, wooden-wheeled factory carts, pulleys and corn mills sit silently; even the signage for the aptly named Pumphouse and Tank House Lanes remains in place. While Victorian factories and their reuse are quite common in Europe, a site of this size and condition is a true anomaly in Canada. Located a short 15-minute walk from the eastern edge of the downtown core, the intersection of King and Parliament was once the epicentre of Toronto's vibrant industrial past.

Of the 100 buildings that made up the original distillery, only 45 remain, the majority of which are of heavy timber, post-and-beam construction with brick or stone walls. And while they might be described as architecturally robust, a consistent stylish flourish and an industrial elegance are revealed in the brick friezes, stone corbelling and wooden fenestration. It is this historical palette and notion of 'found objects' that the architectural team of Tom Payne, Chris Couse and Mark Jaffar capitalised on, or more accurately left intact, to serve as rich backdrops for their minimal yet contemporary interventions.

Programmatically, the 4000-square-metre (4780 square yards) venue contains a variety of performance, workshop, training studios and public spaces, each convertible so as to perform multiple functions. The Baillie Theatre offers Toronto's only thrust stage (where the audience is

---

Opposite

Occupying the simple, red-brick Tank Houses numbers 9 and 10 and the newly-enclosed spaces between them, theatre-goers and performers are treated to a unique ensemble of time, architectural history, culture and performance

discover
Explore

Right
Architect's early rendering exploring an
appropriate expression for the theatre
and public spaces

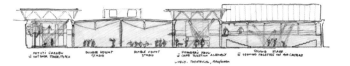

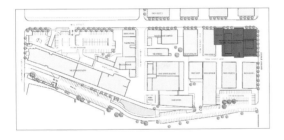

seated on three sides) and can easily be reconfigured to feature traditional proscenium and even theatre-in-the-round. There is also the 220-seat Michael Young Theatre, the 90-seat Roger and Kevin Garland Cabaret space and the 125-seat Tank House Theatre, each with movable partitions and flexible seating configurations to handle a variety of events.

Approached from a distance along Tank House Lane, the experience is unquestionably *industrial-chic*. To resonate with the existing darkened patina, the architects responded with an extended wooden overhang, painted steel grey, to shelter visitors as they move along the cobblestone lane towards the entry lobby. Scallops of downlighting and a projected image of the theatre company's logo on the adjacent Tank House walls enhance the marquee effect.

What was once residual outdoor space between two warehouses is now the main reception area/lobby bar. Capable of hosting intimate fireside performances, the lobby bar represents a paradigm shift in the way the space is programmed. Typically, the lobby is a single-use space, occupied only before the show and during intermission. Here, the lobby is open between performances as an interactive hub for students, professional actors and the public. Spanned by massive Douglas fir timber trusses and cross-beams, the space is left intentionally raw with exposed gusset-plates and bolts. With intervening clerestory glazing, the weighty trusses appear to float over the untreated masonry walls. Of great delight is the plush box seating that frames the recessed stone fireplace. Set with a view on to Tank House Lane, the hearth is a choice spot for a lucky foursome to watch the snow fall during intermission.

Finishes are deliberately industrial and utilitarian. Polished concrete floors further the industrial motif while exposed ceilings create a complex yet consistent visual canopy that weaves through the various performance spaces. Aside from the bar with its lengthy black granite top, the most prominent element in the lobby is the lift tower, sheathed in golden wooden panelling. Wrapping their way upward, open metal stairs are painted steel grey while wooden treads and railings of frosted glass and perforated metal contrast with the textured brick walls. Shooting through overhead, the connecting catwalks are detailed in a similar aesthetic, doubling as mock-mezzanines during intimate performances in the lobby bar. Adding a splash of colour, the original window frames, shutters and friezes are left intact and are painted a warm green, consistent with the original Gooderham colour palette used throughout the district.

To realise such a utopian dream, Soulpepper welcomed significant donations from the city's leading patrons. The Young Family Foundation, after which the theatre is named, contributed close to CA$4 million, while supporters Charles and Marilyn Baillie received naming credits for the 400-seat main stage in recognition of their CA$1 million donation. The troupe has also received generous donations from Roger and Kevin Garland for the development of smaller performance spaces.

With over 175 theatre troupes and nearly 100 dance companies, Toronto is the world's third largest English language theatre community. Under its current director Albert Schultz, Soulpepper is a Toronto-based company dedicated to presenting classic plays. Founded in 1998 by 12 local actors as a summer-only classical ensemble, Soulpepper has grown to become a key aspect of Toronto's theatre scene, and a local alternative to the popular Stratford and Shaw festivals. George Brown College, also in Toronto, is a long-standing learning institution that has been providing theatrical training for over 35 years.

Above
Box seating frames the recessed stone fireplace. Set with a view on to Tank House Lane, the hearth is a choice spot for a lucky foursome to watch the snow fall during the intermission

Left
The project challenges the prototypical models for small theatres by integrating teaching and live performance spaces in one facility, all set within the backdrop of the restored nineteenth-century Gooderham & Worts Distillery District

discover
Explore

Above
Wrapping their way upward, open metal stairs are painted steel grey while golden wooden treads and railings of frosted glass and perforated metal contrast with the textured brick walls

Left
The Mill Street facade incorporates the restored brick facades of the Tank Houses spanned by wooden trusses

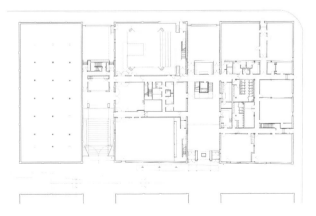

Left
The existing Tank Houses have been retrofitted into theatre and studio spaces, while the areas between them have been turned into public spaces and an outdoor courtyard

Right
The Baillie Theatre offers Toronto's only
thrust stage (where the audience is
seated on three sides) and can easily
be reconfigured to feature traditional
proscenium and even theatre-in-the-
round

Below
Programmatically, the 4000-square-
metre (4780 square yards) venue
contains a variety of public workshop
and performance spaces and training
studios, each entirely convertible so as
to perform multiple functions

discover
Explore

Below
Five massive cubes pierced by refracted spears of light interlock with each other and wrap around the historic 1914 and 1933 stone wings before spilling out onto the Bloor streetscape, to create a new shimmering urban beacon

Right
The winning scheme of offset cubes was actually first set to paper by Libeskind on a ROM café napkin while touring the existing buildings

Royal Ontario Museum

Studio Daniel Libeskind / Bregman + Hamann Architects

Queen's Park Circle, Toronto   2006

For the past 40 years the Royal Ontario Museum (ROM) seemed more like a foreboding fortress – the massive stone edifice and blackened windows largely impenetrable – than a welcoming institution of experience, knowledge and exploration. Today, standing at the corner of Bloor Street and Queen's Park, one of Toronto's most important urban intersections, it is difficult to tell which is more exciting – watching the massive interlocking steel skeleton rise and tilt precariously overhead, or the anticipation of the sculptural jewel that it will soon morph into. Regardless, the museum and, undoubtedly, the city will forever be seen in a shining new light.

Asserting itself as a key protagonist in launching the city's architectural renaissance, Renaissance ROM, is the ambitious expansion initiative designed to reconnect Canada's largest museum with its culturally and architecturally burgeoning host city. In fact, the ROM is extremely well positioned to make this claim, as it is in close proximity to a number of key arts venues also undergoing significant architectural changes including the Royal Conservatory of Music, the renovated Gardiner Museum of Ceramic Art and the Bata Shoe Museum.

Starting from an initial list of 50 international firms, Studio Daniel Libeskind – in joint venture with local architects Bregman + Hamann – was selected after a comprehensive review process that included input from the public, a first-round list of 12, and final short-list of three including Italy's Architetto Andrea Bruno, and Canada's Bing Thom Architects. Commenting on the selection, William Thorsell, ROM Director and Chief Executive Officer writes, 'Daniel Libeskind has been responsible for brilliant and profound works of art and of culture. He possesses that rare quality of bringing an enormous intelligence and thoughtfulness and reflection to a project and then matching it with an equal amount of creativity.'[1]

Entitled The Crystal (actually the Michael Lee-Chin Crystal, so named in honour of its benefactor's generous CA$30 million contribution), the prismatic natural objects found in the ROM's extensive gem and mineralogy galleries inspired the geometric shapes. The concept of offset transparent cubes was actually first set to paper by Libeskind on a ROM café napkin while touring the existing buildings. In actuality, the idea of a fully transparent crystal is slightly misleading, as anodised aluminium will cover 75 per cent of the structure, with the remaining 25 per cent being a random pattern of slices and wedges of transparent glass. Nevertheless, the effect of a shimmering urban beacon is still quite powerful as five massive cubes pierced by refracted spears of light interlock with each other and wrap around the historic 1914 and 1933 stone wings before spilling out onto the Bloor streetscape.

The central and largest crystal defines the museum's entry and acts as the datum from which the collection of gallery and public spaces will radiate, including restored wings devoted to China, Japan and Korea as well as a new gallery for Canadian First Peoples. Titled the Hyacinth Gloria

project
Royal Ontario Museum
100 Queen's Park Circle, Toronto, Ontario

architect
Studio Daniel Libeskind in joint venture with Bregman + Hamann Architects

telephone
+1 416 586 8000

website
www.rom.on.ca

opening hours
Mon – Thurs, Sat – Sun: 10am to 6pm
Fri: 10am to 9:30pm

neighbourhood
at the crossroads of Bloor Street and University Avenue, a neighbourhood of stylish shopping and elegant restaurants and galleries

style
a shimmering urban beacon of five massive aluminium and glass cubes affixed to a grand stone edifice

clientele
tourists and young families, the creative, the intellectual and the curious

signature experience
overlooking the city skyline from the corner table of the Crystal Five Bistro Bar; undoubtedly the best table in the city

other projects
The Jewish Museum Berlin, Berlin; Grand Canal Performing Arts Centre and Galleria, Dublin

Chen Crystal Court, the dramatic multistorey atrium is punctuated by two massive skylights that protrude awkwardly down into the space and direct beams of light to the floor below. Above, a network of perilous catwalks crosses through from the Spirit House, yet another multi-level void space created at the intersection between the massive crystals. Accessed via the Stair of Wonders, Crystals 2, 3 and 4 will host a number of popular galleries including the Age of Dinosaurs, Mammals and Textiles. The dramatic final act though is saved for the top where the Crystal Five Bistro Bar (C5) opens itself up to offer sumptuous meals, fine wine and signature views of the city skyline in the distance.

Beyond providing a fantastic urban spectacle, Libeskind's scheme also works to restore axial sightlines and reprograms existing spaces into new and more appropriate functions. This is what the ROM desperately needed as previous renovations had all but destroyed the original flow between galleries, subdivided its great halls, and buried intricate historic stone details. With four existing galleries newly renovated, the interior is no longer dark and mazelike as windows have been stripped of their blackout paint, ceilings have been pulled down and walls removed to create a beautiful open and naturally lit space. One also begins to understand that Libeskind's Crystal vision is in fact far more comprehensive than simply the assemblage of giant cubes. Inside the newly created Korea and China galleries, visitors are magically transported deep within a giant gemstone as the rediscovered light refracts through the sequence of all-glass parallelogram display cases, whose layout mimics the same jagged knife style as the new building. But this is just the beginning: over 75 per cent of the existing historic galleries will also be renovated in the same style, the largest heritage restoration of its kind in Canada.

One of the most recognisable renovated spaces is the Rotunda, a spectacular arched dome that has served as the main entry since 1933. No longer a crowded and noisy entry, it will be transformed into the Rotunda Café, a magical room where visitors can relax with a book, or simply enjoy the history of the space. Adding to the experience, a number of the original details have been restored including: a pair of oak entrance doors framed by decorative stained-glass windows, inlaid animal motifs to soften the stone floors, and the four hand-carved oak benches designed specifically for the room. Of course, the most spectacular feature is the domed ceiling, covered in Venetian-glass mosaic tiles and animated with intricate figures and historical symbols in rich hues of gold, bronze, vivid reds and blues.

Another familiar space to receive a facelift is the Samuel Hall/Currelly Gallery. Once a dark transitional throughpoint for the major galleries, the majestic hall now flows into the space of the Crystal Court. Fashioned after a grand 1930s hotel lobby, the room features six individual lounge areas with modern Neinkämper furniture and hand-woven carpets designed

Above
Accessed via the Stair of Wonders, Crystals 2, 3 and 4 *(top)* will host a number of popular galleries, while the dramatic multistorey atrium will be punctuated by two protruding skylights *(above)* that will direct beams of light onto the floor below

discover
Explore

Right
Construction photograph of the
complex network of steel beams that
will form the five interlocking crystals

Above
Entitled the Michael Lee-Chin Crystal,
the geometric shapes of the new building were inspired by the natural crystals
found in the ROM's extensive gem and
mineralogy galleries

by Alan Pourvakil giving visitors a place to map out a route or contemplate the day's events.

Created in 1912 and home to nearly six million remarkable and beautiful objects in its collections, the ROM is North America's fifth largest museum and a significant architectural fixture. Featuring Canada's culture and natural history, the ROM also conducts important scientific research, placing it among the world's leading knowledge producers. To fund the ambitious project, the ROM is seeking major investment from both the public and private sectors, including applications to the Provincial Government's SuperBuild fund, the Federal Government, as well as a capital fundraising campaign.

1   Media Release, Royal Ontario Museum, 2005.

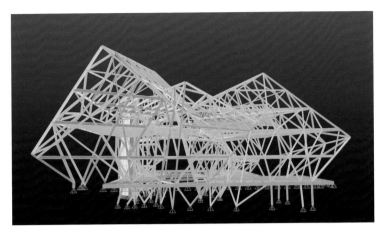

Left
It is difficult to tell which is more exciting – seeing the massive interlocking steel skeleton or anticipating the sculptural jewel that it will soon morph into

Right
From Bloor Street, the crystal forms will collide with the space of the street to create a new urban forecourt and redefine the museum's main entrance

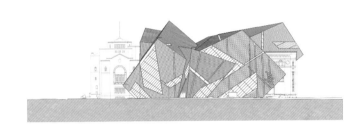

Right
The original eastern facade of the historic museum will remain intact, while the five new crystals will rise behind and create a new entrance off Bloor Street

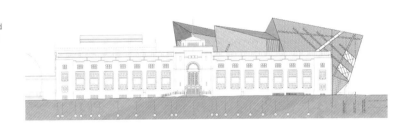

Right
Reflecting forms found in the natural world, the crystalline nature of the new building is immediately apparent when viewed from above

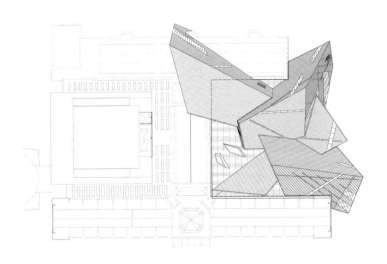

Opposite
The massive steel skeleton of the new building rises against the golden brick of the original museum

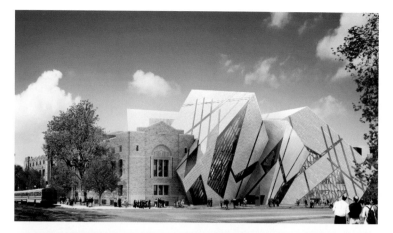

Left
The idea of a fully transparent crystal
is slightly misleading as champagne-
coloured aluminium will cover most of
the structure

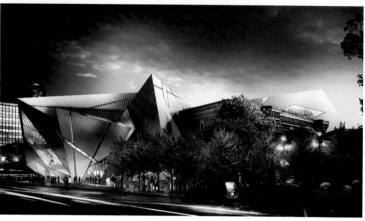

Above
Viewed from the Philosophers' Walk on
Bloor Street, Renaissance ROM is the
ambitious expansion initiative designed
to reconnect Canada's largest museum
with its culturally and architecturally
burgeoning host city

Right
Champagne-coloured anodised aluminium will cover around three-quarters of
the structure, with the remaining quarter
a random pattern of slices and wedges
of transparent glass

discover
Explore

Right

At the project's core is the Spirit House, a multi-level space created at the intersection between the crystals. Rising the full height from basement to roof, the space will be pierced by a network of catwalks crisscrossing at various levels

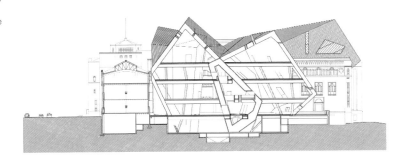

Toronto Waterfront Redevelopment

West 8 / du Toit Allsopp Hillier

Lake Ontario, Toronto   2006

project
Toronto Waterfront Redevelopment
Waterfront between Jarvis Street and
Bathurst Street, Toronto, Ontario

architect
West 8 in joint venture with du Toit
Allsopp Hillier and the Toronto Waterfront
Revitalization Committee

telephone
+1 416 214 1344

website
www.towaterfront.ca

opening hours
not applicable

neighbourhood
where the city core meets the shores
of Lake Ontario

style
a Champs Elysées-style urban
boulevard with a touch of Canadiana
post and beam

clientele
tourists, sports enthusiasts and
Torontonians alike

signature experience
walking, biking or blading uninterrupted
along the 'public row', a wooden,
maple-treed boardwalk from Jarvis
to Bathurst

other projects
West 8: Masterplan for the 2012
Olympic Village, London
du Toit Allsopp Hillier: Confederation
Boulevard, Ottawa ; West Donlands,
Toronto

There is no doubt that Toronto is indeed a *Design City*. But what does this really mean? Of course, the recent explosion of fantastical structures by many of the world's noted architects must surely be enough for us to so confidently make this claim? Granted built forms are a significant measure; being a *Design City*, however, is much more than the product of its buildings or the calibre of the architects that arrive to design them. It is also about what happens in between those buildings, in the 'space of the city' where the public meet and interact on a daily basis. To be a *Design City* then is to understand that quality public open space is a vital urban element and collectively provides for the good of everyone, not just the select few who get goose bumps when standing beside a new Foster or Gehry building.

With the space of the city changing almost daily, the timing is perfect as Toronto is finally taking action on its recent waterfront revitalisation initiative. In reality, our history with the waterfront can be traced back to the city's founder, John Graves Simcoe, who in 1793 advocated the preservation of the water's edge for the benefit of all citizens. Today, the initiative has taken the form of an international design competition. Led by the Toronto Waterfront Revitalization Committee (TWRC), the group unanimously selected Rotterdam landscape architect Adriaan Geuze of West 8, in joint venture with du Toit Allsopp Hillier, a local urban design/architecture firm known for large-scale civic projects. West 8 itself is no stranger to big design as the firm is currently planning a 6-kilometre (3.72 miles) river walk in Madrid. And if this attention isn't enough to sell Toronto's *Design City* status, the waterfront competition attracted some of the world's most innovative designers including London's Foster and Partners and New York's Tod Williams and Billie Tsien.

At the crossroads of building and urban design, the point of the waterfront scheme is to create continuous public access, or more appropriately, connections at all levels. Running the length of the waterfront from Bathurst Street to the southern tip of Jarvis Street is the 'public row', an 18-metre (59 feet) wide wooden and maple-treed boardwalk with seven undulating heavy timber bridges that leap over the existing slip heads. The bridges are significant in that they give pedestrians uninterrupted access along the entire length, but more importantly they speak the vernacular of the heavy timber railway bridges that once dominated the Canadian north. Just inland, Queen's Quay Boulevard will be devoted as much to the pedestrian as it is to cars. Reduced from its unnecessarily oversized four lanes to two, the southern half will be configured as an animated granite esplanade. Already in place, the tram-lines will stay intact and connect the various waterfront villages and landscaped moments including the already successful Queen's Quay Terminal and the new Rees shoreline, remodelled as the Canadian Shield with a kayak and canoe basin.

Left
The team plans to plant thousands of
new maple trees to re-establish the
original summer greenery and autumn
colour spectacle of the waterfront or,
as Geuze calls it, the city's 'green foot'

Below
A composite diagram of the city's major
northbound avenues, or key lines of
cultural continuity

Right
Celebrating the city's 'lines of culture',
several signature moments are created
at the foot of major northward avenues
and at the heads of waterfront slips

Toronto Waterfront Redevelopment

Left

A whimsical folly will be at the base of University Avenue, where a floating bioremediation reef will take the form of the iconic maple leaf

Left

At Portland Slip, the long abandoned Malting Silos will be retrofitted as a water filtration plant, where the ecological processes will be made visible

Below

Queen's Quay Boulevard will be reconfigured as much for pedestrians as for cars, the southern end being reduced from four lanes to two and animated with a new granite esplanade served by the existing tram lanes

discover
Explore

Right
A number of undulating heavy timber bridges will leap over the existing slip heads. More importantly they speak the vernacular of the heavy timber railway bridges that once dominated the Canadian north

Above
Both new and existing structures will be animated at night by dramatic coloured lighting effects

But the notion of connection does not run solely parallel to the water's edge. Celebrating the city's 'lines of culture', several signature moments are created at the foot of major northward avenues. The base of Yonge Street, the longest street in the world, will see a redesigned ferry terminal shuttling the summer masses to the nearby Ward's and Centre Islands. Linking the waterfront with Chinatown, a floating pagoda restaurant will celebrate the culture corridor that is Spadina Avenue. The most whimsical will be at the base of University Avenue, where the floating bioremediation reef in the form of the iconic maple leaf will tip its hat to Queen's Park, the city's political seat. Additionally, the boardwalk will connect to the Martin Goodman Trail system and tie into the West Donlands community, a new mixed-use development for 100,000 people on reclaimed brown lands at the mouth of the Don River.

What the scheme also does is force the city to deal with another festering legacy: the Gardiner Expressway. No doubt Toronto is timid when it comes to large-scale urban design projects, so Geuze's suggestion to demolish the elevated expressway and replace it with a Champs Elysées-style boulevard will certainly raise some eyebrows. For all its grandeur though, there is also a family of small details that add a sense of romance and, literally, light, as the light fixtures and illuminated handrails are inspired by the iconic CN Tower. Throughout the scheme the team also plans to plant thousands of new maple trees to re-establish the original summer greenery and autumn colour spectacle of the waterfront or, as Geuze calls it, the city's 'green foot'.

While the initial competition budget of CA$20 million for the first phase falls short, West 8 has not left the city wanting for innovative design ideas. As whimsical as some of them are, they point to the fact that Toronto indeed has all the right elements of a true *Design City*: a mosaic of diverse cultures, a cosmopolitan metropolis on the water's edge and the momentum to make it happen; a combination no other city in Canada can claim.

Above
The aim of the waterfront scheme is
to create continuous public access and
connections at all levels. Running from
Bathurst Street to the southern end
of Jarvis Street is the 'public row', an
18-metre (59 feet) wide wooden and
maple-treed boardwalk

Left
The boardwalk is based on an 18 metre
width, the minimum spacing for trees to
produce a dense green promenade

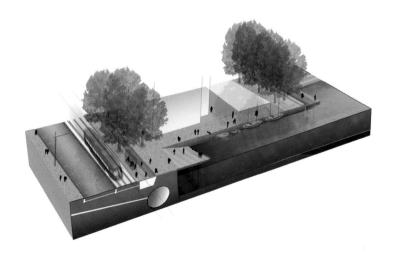

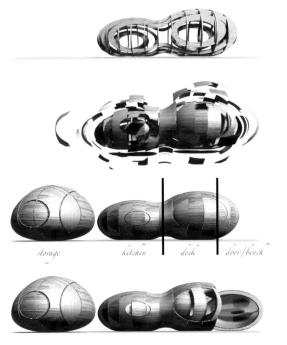

storage   kitchen   desk   door/bench

Above and left
At the base of Spadina Avenue, the design proposes a number of whimsical interventions, including this small fast food pavilion

'I hope that Toronto will continue to express itself and develop itself in design, architecture, and every other way, socially as well to be what it is – one of the world's great cities … It can only be done with a daring architecture and an architecture that takes risks. It's not about just repeating something with a clever facade, but really pushing the boundaries of what the public expects. They don't expect second-rate performances in music or second-rate meals or second-rate wine … and once the bar has been raised, it will never go below.'

Daniel Libeskind, interview with the authors
Toronto, June 2006

Toronto is a city with an increasingly sophisticated palate. Just as the plethora of new architectural and cultural spaces in the city has democratised and brought architecture to the masses, the abundance of restaurant choices across Toronto with their varied menus and designs has made patrons a little more discerning about what they're willing to eat. While the 1970s and '80s were defined by high-end Italian glitz, and the 1990s marked by the emergence of the bistro and organic eateries, today's Toronto is a veritable menu of options. One of the most multicultural cities in the world, the Greater Toronto Area offers over 5000 restaurants serving over 200 different international cuisines. You can just as easily find a restaurant that serves Filipino home cooking as one that serves the finest in French fare. As in most large cities, the immigrant populations have created clusters and neighbourhoods like Koreatown, Little India, and Chinatown which bring together foods and offerings from exotic locales. Celebrations like the popular Taste of the Danforth that draws over a million foodies together in Toronto's Greektown, and the Summerlicious and Winterlicious festivals, help to showcase the talents of the city's restaurateurs.

Décor and ambience play an important role in attracting patrons in the competitive restaurant market. Areas like hip and artsy Queen Street West demand spaces that are fashion-forward and oh-so-cool. Who better to lead this brigade than Ultra Supper Club, the sexy and sumptuous dining/lounge space set among Queen Street's trendy retail and the interactive MuchMusic Canadian headquarters? To the south, in the burgeoning King West Village, other lounge-restaurant spaces like C Lounge and Blowfish have given new life to the former factories and bank buildings lining the street.

Taking the mantra of 'reduce, reuse, recycle' to heart, the Distillery District in Toronto's east end offers an interesting mix of contemporary cuisine in more rustic settings. The Boiler House Restaurant, a soaring wooden cathedral built of 150-year old timber beams, salvaged vintage lighting, concrete and wrought iron, sits on the cobblestone streets of the 13-acre brownfield site. Just west, in the adjacent St Lawrence Market

area, Izakaya offers a quick spot to grab a bowl of hot ramen noodles.
With its exposed brick walls, shoji screens, and rough-hewn blond wood
tables, the feeling is more East meets West, familiar yet new. A few doors
down, at the Jamie Kennedy Restaurant and Wine Bar, design touches of
Canadiana Redux enhance the organic menu through clean, sparse
furnishings and a soft autumnal palette in shades of chocolate, caramel,
and ochre. It seems whatever your taste, you can find it in Toronto.

Blowfish Restaurant + Sake Bar

Johnson Chou Inc

King Street West, Toronto   2003

project
Blowfish Restaurant + Sake Bar
668 King Street West, Toronto, Ontario

architect
Johnson Chou Inc

telephone
+1 416 860 0606

website
www.blowfishrestaurant.com

opening hours
Mon–Sat: 5pm to 2am
Sun: Closed

neighbourhood
hidden inside a nondescript former bank
building along the emerging King Street
West restaurant row

style
a minimal but elegant space which
expertly transforms itself from a classic
dining environment to a late-night stylish
lounge

clientele
stylish locals and sophisticated foodies

signature experience
seated at the glowing bar, enjoying a
chilled saketini followed by a nibble of
succulent Kobe beef sashimi

other projects
TNT Blu Hazelton Lanes, Toronto;
Grip Limited, Toronto

French existentialist Maurice Merleau-Ponty proposed that a single state of being existed between the body and its environment. In contemplating this union he theorised that 'as one enters, a position becomes situation … becomes playground, becomes oneself'.[1] This notion of combining body, space and experience is a process Toronto architect Johnson Chou feels most comfortable in. In fact, Chou's talent for seamlessly morphing together dualities of function when space is at an absolute premium has become his calling card. It is no surprise then that he would shine brightest in Blowfish, a contemporary restaurant set within the aesthetic of a heritage bank building celebrating Asian-fusion cuisine.

Like all fusion cooking, which seeks to create gastronomic delicacies through the synthesis of distinct and often divergent cuisines, Blowfish equally thrives somewhere in the indeterminate architectural zone between modernism and heritage preservation, in the juxtaposition of Eastern and Western architecture resulting in a hybrid space that is at once precious and commonplace, modern and classical. Located in the burgeoning King Street West restaurant district, Chou was presented with some very pragmatic goals: to create a distinct brand with a compelling street appeal, and to restore and enhance the handsome existing stone facades with minimal modern interventions.

From the outside, the apparent solidity of the brick and stone edifice belies the complexity and depth of the layering held within. It is only when you succumb to the lure of the neon glow and pass through the glass threshold and interpret the layers first hand that the multiplicity of the space is fully revealed. The notion of duality is pervasive in everything from layout to the details. Inside, four main spaces function in unison and like so many of Chou's projects, they are imbued with theatrical overtones. A lounge positioned near the entrance receives guests while providing uninterrupted views of the massive onyx, wood and hot-rolled steel bar running the entire length of the room and set aglow by vibrant back-lighting. Along the front wall, a tan leather banquette illuminated by coloured recessed lighting appears to hover above the dark wood floor, while chrome lounge tables reflect the dim ambient glow and add a touch of theatrical sparkle. Framing the rear of the room, the arched sushi bar sits on an elevated platform. With unobstructed views of the restaurant, the sushi chef retains his exalted position as ceremonial master of the house as both viewer and viewed.

The most salient expression of the dualities of fusion is the division of the space by the freestanding wire mesh screen. First isolating the bar, the screen then wraps itself overhead to define the space of the dining area. As day turns to dusk, the changing light creates a phase shift from transparent to opaque and, like a theatrical scrim, the shoji-esque screen serves as an enigmatic vehicle for sensory temptation, providing enticing yet suggestive glimpses of the activities on either side. Again patrons

Above
From the outside, the apparent solidity of the brick and stone edifice belies the complexity and depth of the layering held within

Right
Lured by the neon glow, patrons pass through the glass threshold into the multi-layered space

Left
The contemporary restaurant celebrates
Asian-fusion cuisine within the aesthetic
of a heritage bank building

Below
There are uninterrupted views of
patrons seated at the massive onyx,
wood and hot-rolled steel bar running
the entire length of the room and set
aglow by vibrant back-lighting

Right
A freestanding wire mesh screen isolates the bar and wraps itself overhead to define the space of the dining area – this modern, *shoji*-esque screen accentuated by the juxtaposition of highly ornate custom-designed crystal chandeliers

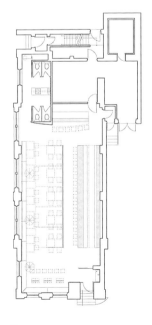

Above
The tight plan is organised around a sequence, starting with the lounge at the front and moving through the bar and dining area, past the sushi bar and on to the unisex washrooms at the rear

reside somewhere between observer and participant. This obvious duality is accentuated even further by the juxtaposition of highly ornate custom-designed crystal chandeliers against the modern metal screen. Conceived as a modern adaptation of traditional French luminaires, the chandeliers are purposely opulent yet extended and languorous so as to have a symbolic and ethereal presence in the room.

Yet another and somewhat playful example of hybridity is the unisex washrooms. Hidden from plain view behind the extended curved wall of the sushi bar, two pairs of private stalls share a common island vanity unit and basin. Fabricated from perforated stainless steel, the island is fully accessible from both sides for either gender, although it is divided by a cantilevered mirror with integrated lighting. Descending from the ceiling, sets of stainless-steel pipes function as motion-activated taps. While pragmatically the unisex design eliminates the dreaded washroom queue for women, socially, it creates yet another opportunity for impromptu interaction or spontaneous performances.

Not unlike fusion cuisine, Johnson Chou seamlessly spans creative disciplines and readily admits that the borders are fundamentally interchangeable. 'I see it all being linked', he says, 'it's all about narrative and bringing it all together … materials, space and people … each a necessary element in realising a unified whole'. If, as Chou describes, his work is a constant critique of the built environment, it makes one wonder, is he describing Blowfish or Toronto?

1   Maurice Merleau-Ponty, *The Primacy of Perception*, Northwestern University Press, Evanston, 1964

Left
The space improvises with a palette
ranging from finely-detailed joinery and
tiny glass mosaic tiles to rough-hewn
150-year-old timber beams

Boiler House Restaurant

Mackay|Wong Strategic Design / Eagar+Co Architecture+Design

Mill Street, Toronto   2003

With increasing frequency, the preservation of brownfield or historic buildings is being viewed as a popular antidote to declining urban neighbourhoods. It is no surprise then that 'going green' and the notion of sustainable design have become popular measures for designers and clients in determining a building's success. Often calculated in quantifiable terms such as 'payback period', is it possible that sustainability has been co-opted as 'preservation for commercial incentive'? Should sustainability instead be a qualitative and intentional methodology for design, fabrication and operation?

The owners of the Distillery District thought so and gave the design team the brief to reuse, recycle and plan innovatively, thus resulting in a place that not only celebrates the material essence and architectural spirit of the place, but also through the process of construction educates and gives back to the community.

A very ambitious mandate indeed; but then again the restored nineteenth-century Gooderham & Worts Distillery District is itself a very ambitious project. The largest and most intact brownfield site in Canada, the district is a wonderful collection of over 40 fully preserved, Victorian timber and brick warehouse and whisky production facilities. Amid the collage of heritage buildings that date between 1860 and 1900, there is a cooperage, a pumphouse, rack houses, stables and barrelhouses. Today, at the hands of Cityscape Development, the site has morphed into Toronto's first true pedestrian quarter; an arts and leisure community of resident artists and studios, cafés, galleries and restaurants.

Most of these buildings were constructed in a time when it made sense to produce everything you needed on site, from the barrels to age the whisky to the labels on the bottles. In fact, this improvisational and utilitarian approach became the same *modus operandi* for the new restaurant as well. Mackay|Wong, a Toronto design firm and project team leader, invited Eagar+Co Architecture+Design to collaborate with them in achieving the client's vision of adaptive reuse. Working with heritage preservation specialists ERA Architects, a collage of artifacts found on site during construction were reclaimed and cast into new uses. However, fully understanding the depth of architectural memory evident in the site, remnants selected first had to be proven programmatically relevant and functionally useful. Something to be engaged with and never nostalgic or trendy, history is not put on display but, instead, put to work.

Walking into the double-height brick shell of the former rack house, the experience is akin to entering a soaring wooden cathedral. Immediately apparent is the massive main bar, a concrete hulk that runs

project
Boiler House Restaurant
55 Mill Street, Toronto, Ontario

architect
Mackay|Wong Strategic Design in joint collaboration with Eagar+Co Architecture+Design

telephone
+1 416 203 2121

website
www.boilerhouse.ca

opening hours
Tues – Sat: dinner service 5pm to close
Sat: brunch 11am to 3pm

neighbourhood
in the Distillery District, a historic industrial relic of Victorian buildings set on 13 acres in downtown Toronto

style
recycled materials and modest contemporary design combine to create an industrial but elegant setting

clientele
casual diners, local tourists and jazz fans enjoy a soothing blend of music and hearty fare

signature experience
sitting in the outdoor patio, with cobblestones underfoot and strains of jazz filling the lazy afternoon air

other projects
Mackay|Wong: Wayne Gretzky's Restaurant, Toronto; WEGZ Stadium Bar, Toronto
Eagar+Co Architecture+Design: Sistemalux Showroom, Toronto

Left
Entering into the double-height brick shell of the former rack house, the experience is akin to stepping inside a soaring wooden cathedral

the full length of the room, capped by a continuous 75 mm (3 inch) thick plank of salvaged knotty spruce. In a miniature version of the massive storage racks of the adjacent cask building where thousands of whisky barrels once sat aging, the bar features a full-height, three-dimensional grid of rough-hewn timber where hundreds of wine bottles are stored. In a similar move, a stretch of heavy wooden slabs line up and wrap around individual tables and form intimate mini-cubbies for two.

The dining area shares the same industrial feel of the bar. Tables are hewn from recycled wooden slabs while the sky-blue leather bench seating provides a decidedly modern feel when paired with crisp white tablecloths. Completing the room, the matching blue back wall glows behind a filigree of vertical slats, painted black. Overhead, salvaged vintage lighting fixtures illuminate a metal catwalk detailed with wrought-iron spindles, also found on site, while underfoot the polished concrete floor provides a consistent datum.

Many of the details were made with reclaimed artifacts. The real art of sustainability is embraced and evidenced in the site's (hi)story of creation as an accretive, learned process of incremental development. Rather than pre-planning every detail, the district's restoration team was empowered with creating and fabricating the restaurant's interior details during construction. Improvising with a palette that ranged from finely-detailed joinery to rough-hewn 150-year-old timber beams, each detail has become imbued with a sensitivity and language that could only be translated through the individual hands of an artisan responding intuitively to whatever was on hand at the time. Of course, this desire to learn and then pass on the knowledge is ultimately what sustainability is all about.

Above
The bar features a full-height, three-dimensional grid of rough-hewn timber where hundreds of wine bottles are stored, identified by original distillery reference markings

Right
The building sits within the Distillery District, a wonderful collection of over 40 fully preserved, Victorian timber and brick warehouse and whisky production facilities

Boiler House Restaurant

Immediately apparent in the lounge area
is the massive main bar, a concrete hulk
that runs the full length of the room, capped by an equally impressive continuous
75 mm (3 inch) thick plank of salvaged
knotty spruce

Below
The blue back wall of the dining area
glows behind a filigree of black vertical
slats, while salvaged light fixtures illuminate a metal catwalk detailed with
wrought-iron spindles, also found on
site. Underfoot, the polished concrete
floor provides a consistent datum

Il Fornello Restaurant

Giannone Associates Architects Inc
Church Street, Toronto   2005

project
Il Fornello Restaurant
491 Church Street, Toronto, Ontario

architect
Giannone Associates Architects Inc

telephone
+1 416 944 9052

website
www.ilfornello.com

opening hours
Daily: from 11.30 am
Sat – Sun: brunch from 11.30 am

neighbourhood
Church and Wellesley, the flamboyant,
colourful heart of Toronto's gay village

style
theatrical, as the chameleon-like
space morphs from modern details
to whimsical hot pink accents

clientele
the alternative and style-conscious

signature experience
eyeing the eye-candy during patio
season from deep within the aubergine
stage

other projects
Bar One Restaurant, Toronto; Parkdale
Collegiate Library, Toronto

'Il Fornello' means 'little oven' in Italian. As a restaurant moniker, it conjures up images of homemade pasta and pizza served by grey-haired nonnas in their tomato-stained aprons. Who would have thought it would also be the name for a flamboyant, colourful eatery deep in the heart of Toronto's gay village?

Since 1986, the Il Fornello chain of Italian restaurants has distinguished itself on the Toronto dining scene as a source of casual Italian fare at a moderate cost. With 10 locations throughout the Greater Toronto area and the suburbs of Richmond Hill and Oakville, Il Fornello is known more for its sumptuous pizzas cooked in wood-burning ovens than for its adventurous architecture. With the latest location, however, on Church Street between Wellesley and Carleton Streets, there needed to be a definite new design approach to appeal to the sensibilities of the alternative (and style-conscious) clientele. Giannone Associates Architects Inc, a firm known for its attention to detail and a unique integrative approach to create fully immersive experiences, was up to the challenge. Ralph Giannone, together with partner Pina Petricone, has created a fitting space for one of the most exciting neighbourhoods in Toronto.

Toronto's gay community is a vibrant and lively one. The village is an ever-bustling nexus of social activity, playing host to events such as the Annual Gay Pride Parade, the third largest celebration of gay culture in North America. An abundance of retail, home décor and restaurant spaces can be found in this historic neighbourhood in east Toronto, adjacent to the St James Cemetery and the leafy homes of Cabbagetown.

Paying homage to the social setting in which it exists, Il Fornello is the perfect place to see or be seen. In Toronto, summertime is also known as 'patio season', a time when Torontonians can shed their winter layers and eat al fresco in the temporary storefront patios assembled by the city's restaurants. Il Fornello does this one better, with a chameleon-like space that flips between outdoor patio and enclosed dining space with the change of the seasons. This transformation comes by way of the rolling storefront, a wall-to-wall, floor-to-ceiling structure consisting of a single pane of glass affixed to an aubergine metal frame. The frame can roll 5.5 metres (18 feet) along a sub-track embedded in the wall cavity, bringing the restaurant almost to the pavement edge. This spatial play creates an interesting experience for patrons inside and out. Sitting in the restaurant, the aubergine frame physically frames the exterior view. From the outside looking in, the frame borders an animated scene of diners and interesting design details. With the patio raised on a grey travertine-clad podium just above street level, the feeling of being an actor on a stage observed by passers-by is heightened.

The interior is marked by a whimsical but modern aesthetic. Modular loungers clad in fuchsia and grey fabrics line the patio. Quirky details like the hot pink candle holders inset into the wall niches, the salmon pink

eat *Enjoy*

Right
With the latest location on Church Street, there needed to be a definite new design approach to appeal to the sensibilities of the alternative (and style-conscious) clientele

Left
The rolling storefront allows for a chameleon-like space that flips between outdoor patio and enclosed dining area with the change of the seasons

Above
With striking precision, rich sapele wood panels run up the angled walls and along the ceiling, swooping down in a bold kink which traverses the room in a slight diagonal

Left

Quirky details like the hot pink candle holders inset into the wall niches, the salmon pink pillows and the random plum-coloured side tables make this a cheery place to converse with friends or eye the eye-candy walking by

Left

Washroom doors, lined with mirrors along one side of the hallway and laminated with oversized photos of Italian life on the other, reflect endlessly and lend a whimsical feel to the space

Right
Fully aware of its social setting, Il Fornello
is the perfect place to see or be seen.

Below
A wall faced in gold satin aluminium
panelling bounces the reflections of
patrons seated at the pink leather bar

pillows and the random plum-coloured side tables make this a cheery place to converse with friends or eye the eye-candy walking by. The lack of mullions on the front glazing and the continuation of the travertine flooring underfoot tie this lounge space nicely with the dining space beyond. Covering the length of most of the southern wall is gold satin aluminium panelling which provides a subtle iridescent quality. Reflections of the patrons seated at the pink leather bar bounce off this gilded surface, interrupted only by precise vertical seams and graphic cut-outs.

Moving further indoors, you are struck by the geometry of the long, narrow shoe-box space. A slim white reception desk and miniature shadow box project from a niche in the wall, creating a Mondrian-esque composition. Rich sapele wood panels wrap the entire dining area – the feeling is angular and dramatic. With striking precision, the wood runs up the angled walls and along the ceiling, swooping down in a bold kink which traverses the room in a slight diagonal. The strong lines are accentuated by the repetitive seams, the rows of low-voltage spotlights, and the orderly grid of ceramic plates lining the back wall.

The restaurant is orderly in layout as well, with spaces becoming more intimate as you venture further inside. It flows from the front lounge area, by the open bar, past the inviting banquettes and through to the cosy dining tables. Recessed niches, painted a hot pink, are used throughout the room. Various objects are nestled inside, from plasma televisions to mirrored stands and decorative Majolica vases, providing stimulating hits of colour and reflection.

Tucked away, hidden at the end of the golden wall, is the most intimate of spaces. Where the rest of the restaurant is lively and social, this washroom area is decidedly moody. Large paddles, the kind used to lift pepperoni pizzas out of wood-burning ovens, are set against a stark white wall. Low-voltage spotlights, recessed into the red-tiled communal sink area, offer the only source of light. The exteriors of the washroom doors, lined with mirrors along one side of the hallway and laminated with oversized photos of Italian life on the other, reflect endlessly and create an odd fun-house quality. Like the backstage of a theatre, it provides the perfect spot to escape to when tired of seeing and being seen.

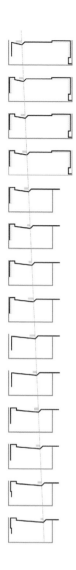

Above
As the sapele wood ceiling moves along its course, it kinks and folds to create a dynamic and fluid wrap

Above
Spaces become more intimate as you venture further inside, flowing from the front lounge area, by the open bar, past the inviting banquettes and through to the cosy dining tables

Left
Various objects are nestled inside hot pink niches, from plasma televisions to mirrored stands and decorative Majolica vases, providing stimulating hits of colour and reflection

102

eat
Enjoy

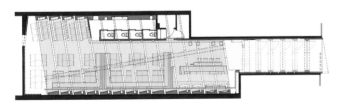

Above
Moving indoors you are struck by the length of the narrow shoe-box space and the knife-cut geometries of the wooden wrap ceiling

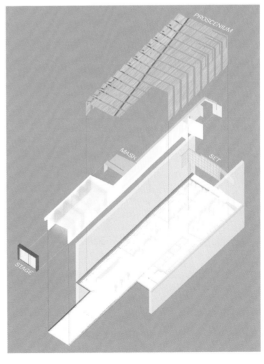

Right
Architect's rendering illustrating the main elements of the scheme including the dramatic wood ceiling and the retractable storefront

Izakaya

II BY IV Design Associates Inc
St Lawrence Market, Toronto   2005

project
Izakaya
   69 Front Street East, Toronto, Ontario

architect
   II BY IV Design Associates Inc

telephone
   +1 416 703 8658

website
   www.izakaya.ca

opening hours
   Mon – Sat: 11:30am to 11:30pm
   Sun: 5pm to 10:30pm

neighbourhood
   alongside the many casual restaurants
   in the St Lawrence Market neighbourhood

style
   a fusion of traditional Asian details
   and dark ebony shoji screens with
   blond-wood tables and contemporary
   oversized graphics

clientele
   office workers in search of a quick lunch
   or after-work casual dinner

signature experience
   simply enjoying a steaming hot bowl of
   ramen noodles while seated at one of
   the communal tables

other projects
   Holt's Café, Toronto; York Event Theatre,
   Toronto

In Japan, a red lantern hanging outside the door of a restaurant typically means an inexpensive hot meal, a few casual drinks and an informal atmosphere. Known as an *izakaya*, the term is actually a compound word with 'i' and 'sakaya' and loosely translates into 'sake shop'. In reality, these ubiquitous urban diners cater to everyone from harried after-work salarymen to twenty-somethings looking for a place to hang out and grab a quick bowl of *ramen* – basically, it is the Japanese equivalent of the urban pub. While you might be hard pressed to find many red lanterns hanging in the streets of Toronto, if you happen to be hungry in the St Lawrence Market, and see a massive red orb glowing against the restored brick of a historic nineteenth-century warehouse, you have probably found the city's equivalent.

Unlike the easily identifiable British counterpart, there really is no one signature style that can be used to describe an *izakaya*. Instead, it is more about an attitude to food and an enjoyment of atmosphere. The challenge was how to insert a traditional Japanese eatery into a Victorian warehouse using contemporary design style. No problem if you are II BY IV Design, architects of a number of distinctive projects including the upcoming Museum Shop and Crystal 5 Bistro Bar at the Royal Ontario Museum. In fact, the lack of a distinctive design brief was actually a blessing, as the very absence of a signature style is rapidly becoming their calling card.

Toronto has a slightly bipolar, if not sometimes manic, appreciation of design; we love our brick, yet we can never seem to get enough of modern finishes. But this was all the brief the designers needed as they fused traditional Asian 'rising sun' details and dark ebony *shoji* screens with blond wood tables, colourful red and gold accents, and contemporary oversized graphics. To say the project proceeded blind is actually not true, as owners John Sinopoli and Eric Joyal each had brushes with Eastern culture. As executive chef, John spent over a year teaching English as a second language to support his self-directed crash course in Japanese cooking, while Eric learned first-hand the art of sushi-less dining during a four year stint in London. Together they deliver the expected staples of *gyoza* and *ramen* in slightly larger than tapas-sized portions.

Moving through the bright red door, the mood is immediately set – dramatic yet also serene. Just inside, in the crush area, a giant glass panel imprinted with pixellated images of cherry blossoms and wrapped in a filigree of natural tree branches serves as the first of many decorative foils controlling our movement within the loft-like space. Looking on, it is almost as if we are standing at the edge of the tree-line having come upon a welcoming clearing in the woods. Again, the giant red orb looming

Right
Known as an izakaya, a red lantern hanging outside the door of a restaurant typically means an inexpensive hot meal, a spot for casual drinks and an informal atmosphere

Right
Izakaya is an intriguing blend of traditional Japanese eatery in a Victorian warehouse with a contemporary design aesthetic

Izakaya

Left
Moving through the bright red door, the mood is immediately dramatic yet serene

Above
In the crush area, a giant glass panel imprinted with pixellated images of cherry blossoms wrapped in a filigree of natural tree branches serves as the first of many decorative foils controlling movement within the loft-like space

Right
A giant red orb looms overhead while decorative wall-mounted bundles of chopsticks and soup bowls turn every-day cooking tools into playful collages of utensil-art

Right
Iconic images of geisha, sumo wrestlers
eating and Zen gardens add another
layer of detail

Above
The Japanese equivalent of the urban
pub, an izakaya caters to everyone from
harried downtown workers to twenty-
somethings looking for a place to grab
a quick bowl of ramen noodles

overhead reminds us of its roots in the Japanese motherland, while decorative wall-mounted bundles of chopsticks and soup bowls turn everyday food instruments into playful collages of utensil art. Beyond the screen, the first of two dining areas lays itself out with rows of light-ash tables and playful polycarbonate stools. The next foil in the space is the main bar, a dark mass of chocolate-brown zebra wood and honed black slate. Behind, the full-height *shoji*-esque screen of Macassar ebony veneer and frosted glass highlights the wine collection set deep within a red rising-sun detail. Overhead, four hand-made Philippine bird's-nest pendants provide a warm golden glow.

Eating at a true *izakaya* is as much about the food as it is about simply getting to know your neighbour. Less so the norm in traditional North American restaurants, the dining area encourages this by providing six massive communal tables that seat 12 on long wooden benches. And while the elegant wooden benches and backless chrome bar stools encourage a fast turnover, smaller tables for two line the perimeter and indulge patrons who are not feeling very social. Nevertheless, these small niches are backlit with turquoise LED lighting and draw attention to themselves and the texture of the restored brick walls. Above, the graphic theme continues as oversized white lanterns stencilled with images of people enjoying all things noodle drop from the black ceiling. Finishing the space is yet another layered screen, this time with iconic images of geisha, sumo wrestlers, and Zen gardens. Throughout, no detail is left unattended as the kitchen servery features faux gold-leaf vinyl wallcovering and glossy black wall tiles. Of course, with all this interaction, privacy is also considered, as each of the four unisex washrooms has a different wall treatment, from traditional bamboo through to grasscloth and black mosaic tile.

For all its graphic drama and wonderfully aged brick, it is only when you step back and look around that you realise that Izakaya is very much an authentic Japanese experience. From fluid spaces and glowing translucent screens to the simple act of eating food with friends, it is no surprise that Izakaya won the Best International Restaurant Design Award at the 2005 FX Design show in London, and is also on toronto.com's critic's choice for top 10 restaurants in the city. At the end of the working day, Izakaya makes good on its promise of delivering Japanese soul food in true *Design City* style.

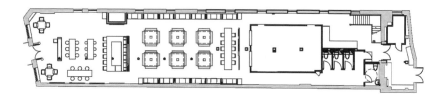

Left
The long narrow room is subdivided by
glowing translucent screens. Six massive
communal tables seat 12, while smaller
tables for two line the perimeter

Right
Sharing is encouraged by the six massive communal tables that seat 12 on long wooden benches

Above
Behind the bar, a *shoji*-esque screen of Macassar ebony veneer and frosted glass highlights the wine collection, while oversized white lanterns stencilled with images of people enjoying all things noodle drop from the black ceiling

Left
The designers fused traditional Asian 'rising sun' details and dark ebony *shoji* screens with blond wood tables, colourful red and gold accents, and contemporary oversized graphics

Jamie Kennedy
Restaurant and Wine Bar

Levitt Goodman Architects
St Lawrence Market, Toronto   2005

Natural. Unpretentious. Fresh. These words describe the cuisine of Jamie Kennedy, one of Canada's most celebrated chefs, but just as fittingly describe his newest abode. The Jamie Kennedy Restaurant and the adjacent Wine Bar provide a casual backdrop for a night of relaxation, gastronomic delight, and conversation. Foodies and design fans alike will eat up the delights that this chef has on offer.

Set in the bustling St Lawrence Market district near Front Street and Church Street, an area teeming with restaurants, lofts and live theatre, the Restaurant and Wine Bar can easily be missed. Barely visible from the street, at the base of a row of old Victorian buildings, you enter into a smallish but welcoming space. Designed by Levitt Goodman Architects, a firm well known for their renovation projects, the rooms are relaxed and unfussy. At once, you feel at home. An abundance of light woods and an autumnal palette of chocolate, caramel, and ochre create a slightly rustic feel. It's a pleasant contrast to Kennedy's last digs at the Royal Ontario Museum, a sleeker lunch-only venue which was closed due to the Daniel Libeskind redesign currently under way at the Museum.

On one side is the Jamie Kennedy Wine Bar, a long and narrow space with a handful of tables for two near the front entry. The wine bar itself, an 8-metre (26.25 feet) slab of 75mm (3 inch) thick Parallam, a composite wood by-product more typically used for structural beams, takes up almost the entire length of one side. Random shadow boxes punctuate a wall of   stacked wine bottles behind the bar, highlighted by the soft glow of the simple white-shaded pendant lights which hang overhead. The bar is an impressive sculpture, milled and polished into a silky smooth finish. It is the perfect spot to enjoy one of the tantalising yet inexpensive dishes on the Wine Bar's tapas menu, which offers appetiser-sized dishes using only the season's freshest ingredients. In keeping with Jamie Kennedy's slow-food philosophy, no reservations are taken for dinner and patrons are encouraged to linger and enjoy a glass of wine suggested by the capable sommelier.

Tucked in the opposite corner is an L-shaped bar which overlooks the open kitchen, giving diners a view of the master chef and sous chefs at work. Row upon row of mason jars filled with Kennedy's own homemade vegetable and fruit preserves create a rainbow display in hues of gold, russet, olive, and crimson – an eye-catching decoration in an otherwise functional space. To keep the cuisine at the forefront, the rest of the furnishings in the Wine Bar are minimal. Simple oak tables and clean-lined chairs are clustered near the entry while a light hardwood floor and neutral paint or brick covered walls envelop the space.

project
Jamie Kennedy Restaurant and Wine Bar
9 Church Street, Toronto, Ontario

architect
Levitt Goodman Architects Ltd

telephone
+1 416 362 1957

website
www.jkkitchens.com

opening hours
Wine Bar
Tues – Sat: 11.30am to 11pm
Restaurant
Mon – Sun: 5pm to 11pm

neighbourhood
tucked away among the restaurants and cafés that dot the St Lawrence Market area

style
relaxed wine bar coupled with casual kitchen chic. A modern mix of textured felt, oak tables, and warm Canadian touches

clientele
foodie neophytes and devoted fans of star chef and restaurateur Jamie Kennedy

signature experience
looking past the colourful mason jar display of pickled fruits and vegetables to see the master chef at work

other projects
Liberty Grand, Toronto; Rockaway Glen Golf and Country Club, St Catharines, Ontario

Opposite
The wine bar, an 8-metre (26.25 feet) slab of Parallam, a composite wood by-product more typically used for structural beams, stretches almost the length of the room

Left
Random shadow boxes punctuate a
wall of wine behind the bar, highlighted
by the soft glow of the simple white-
shaded pendant lights which hang
overhead

The same casual vibe continues into the attached Jamie Kennedy Restaurant. Used formerly as an event venue, it has been transformed into a complementary dining space offering a more conventional à-la-carte menu. A large rectangular booth made of layers of thick plush felt is centred in the room. Acting as both partition and sound barrier, the booth offers built-in banquette seating clad in burnt orange leather and wrapped in a deep light-wood frame. Lucky patrons can debate the intricacies of Kennedy's dishes and his innovative use of ingredients while lounging in this cocoon-like space.

Sparse and clean tables are found throughout, set with simple white place settings and the occasional green accent for a touch of humour. Glass orb lights above provide subtle reflection and bathe the tables in a warm light. Sheer curtain panels in orange and grey line the windows overlooking Church Street, giving the room a hazy glow in the afternoon sun. A large oversized print of a handwritten menu is used as a piece of culinary folk art. The room is unadorned, save for these few furnishings. Kennedy, a passionate advocate of locally grown organic produce, is content to let the food shine on its own. With another venture opened in 2006 at the revamped Gardiner Museum of Ceramic Art, and a restaurant and café featuring ingredients grown on-site in the works as part of the Toronto Brick Works redevelopment, Kennedy will have ample opportunity to attract new converts to his philosophy on food.

Above
An abundance of light woods and an
autumnal palette of chocolate, caramel,
and ochre create a slightly rustic feel

Left
To keep the cuisine at the forefront, the
furnishings in the Wine Bar are minimal
with simple oak tables, white linen, and
clean-lined chairs

Right
Sheer curtain panels in orange and grey
line the windows overlooking Church
Street, giving the room a hazy glow in
the afternoon sun

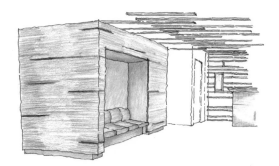

Left
Architect's sketch of the plush felt
banquettes

Right
Row upon row of mason jars filled with Kennedy's own homemade vegetable and fruit preserves create a rainbow display in hues of gold, russet, olive and crimson – an eye-catching decoration in an otherwise functional space

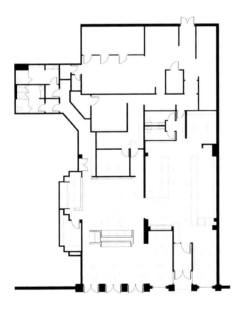

Left
Located on the ground floor of a row of Victorian buildings, the layout is tight but welcoming, with the L-shaped wine bar being the main focal and social point

Left
Acting as both partition and sound barrier, the booth made of plush layers of felt offers built-in banquette seating

Ultra Supper Club

munge//leung: design associates
Queen Street West, Toronto   2004

project

Ultra Supper Club
314 Queen Street West, Toronto, Ontario

architect
munge//leung: design associates

telephone
+1 416 263 0330

website
www.ultrasupperclub.com

opening hours
Mon – Sat: 6pm to close

neighbourhood
in the Queen West neighbourhood, an area dominated by trendy retail, cheap eats, club-kid clientele, and the interactive MuchMusic Canadian headquarters

style
sophisticated dining with a sexy night-club vibe. A stylish blend of reclaimed brick walls, reflective surfaces, and hot pink accents

clientele
a glamorous crowd of visiting celebrities, trendsetters, and social elite

signature experience
sipping on a martini, enjoying the views of Toronto's skyline from Ultra's rooftop patio

other projects
Onda Wine Lounge (Mirage Hotel), Las Vegas, USA; Salad King, Toronto

How do you create a successful restaurant in a competitive market like Toronto? If you are nightclub king Charles Khabouth, you don't – you redefine the genre. Together with partner Brenda Lowes and long-standing design collaborators *munge//leung*, Khabouth has envisioned and created a unique dining room/lounge that has revitalised the Toronto social scene.

On the bones of the venerable Bamboo Restaurant, the team has shaped a sumptuous space that is sexy, lush, and fashion-forward. This is the Queen West neighbourhood, a stretch of the city dominated by trendy retail, cheap eats, club-kid clientele, and the live-in-the-street feel of the interactive MuchMusic Canadian headquarters. Who knew that this former wicker factory could be transformed into the latest playground for the city's social elite?

A pair of massive Indonesian carved wooden doors defines the entry at the street. Venture forth into the calmness of the inner courtyard, down a stone pathway lined with concrete planters, mood lighting, and a striking geometric cedar screen. Behind this partition, a soaring cedar wall extends upward, wrapping around the cosy exterior patio while providing structural support to the rooftop patio above. A chandelier of mini white lights overhead adds sparkle to the clear night sky.

At the hostess station, translucent acrylic panels embedded with reeds give a glimpse of the extravagance within. And what a space it is. Designed by Alessandro Munge and Sai Leung, who trained at the hip of Yabu Pushelberg (the Canadian design darlings responsible for W New York and Tiffany's Fifth Avenue), Ultra is ultra hot. The wicker accents and grass-hut feel of the old Bamboo have given way to velvet ottomans, pin-striped banquettes and red-hot accessories.

With raised 4.25-metre (14 feet) ceilings, the room has a lofty and open feel. The few walls are skinned in a veneer of yellow reclaimed brick, providing a rough foil to the sleekness of the many reflective surfaces. Exotic ebony-stained hardwood underfoot visually links all the zones. A random smattering of floating glass boxes displaying bold accessories and sculptural artefacts gives visual pause. The palette is rich and masculine with ochre, chocolate, and charcoal dominating the space.

In the elevated dining area, large U-shaped banquettes offer the perfect perch to observe the scene. Visiting celebrities are likely ensconced at one of these seats, spacious enough to fit six of their closest friends and outfitted in a snazzy striped fabric. Glass half-walls provide subtle separation from the more active spaces (and the hoi polloi) below while luminous Japanese-inspired lanterns, hung low, maintain a certain intimacy.

Opposite
Venture forth into the calmness of the inner courtyard, down a stone pathway lined with concrete planters, mood lighting, and a striking geometric cedar screen

eat
Enjoy

Rignt
Near the entrance, a trapezoidal bar
made of a unique patterned stone
marks the lounge area

Below
A soaring cedar wall extends upward,
wrapping around the cosy exterior patio
while providing structural support to the
rooftop patio above. A chandelier of
mini white lights overhead adds sparkle
to the clear night sky

Above
Translucent acrylic walls embedded with
reeds give a glimpse of the extravagance
within the main space

Opposite
Pink is repeated throughout the lounge,
from the oversized damask suspended
from the ceiling, to the pink shag carpet
and satin pillows and cushions

Over the main dining area, flickering candle chandeliers, all mirrored stainless steel and glass, cast a sexy glow. Here, the custom designed tables and chairs are smaller in scale and provide ample room for 100 diners. A lucky few get to claim a seat in one of the four dining pods, cosy tables encircled in diaphanous full-height drapery panels.

Near the entrance, a trapezoidal bar made of a striking patterned stone marks the lounge area. Even more striking is the lighting fixture overhead – teardrop shaped vases with flowers intact are suspended from clear wires inside a massive plastic cylinder. It is a radiant delight. The transparency of the fixture stands in contrast to the bold coloration of the mirrored grid of hot pink niches behind the bar. Pink is repeated throughout the lounge: in the oversized damask suspended from the ceiling, with hues of tangerine, pink, and red; in the fun pink shag carpet; in the satin pillows and cushions. Coupled with the low-slung black velour loungers and lacquered Chinese day beds, the room has a definite Asian vibe. Three mirrored pilasters anchor the space, bouncing light and images of the beautiful people at play.

The same reflective feel continues in the washrooms. A glitzy lighting fixture of green and clear crystal droplets spans the length of the countertop, providing a shiny focal point. Silver and black wallpaper and wall-to-wall mirrors sheathe the space. Outside the washrooms, a cosy bar lounge provides a quiet gathering place. Again, glowing pink niches behind the mirrored bar give a welcome hit of colour.

Where the décor of the main dining and lounge spaces is plush and opulent, the outdoor rooftop patio is almost minimal in comparison. Clad in a white on white scheme, the patio is undoubtedly the best place to check out the action on bustling Queen Street below. With private cabana-type spaces, the nod to the Miami Beach style of decorating is evident. Since Ultra, other spots have tried to replicate this South Beach blend of style and sexiness, notably C Lounge with its rooftop swimming pool and swaying palm trees. But Ultra still does it best – with a wide open space to see and be seen and a clientele heavy on celebrity, Ultra is the perfect urban oasis.

Left
Luminous Japanese-inspired lanterns, hung low, maintain a certain intimacy in the dining area

Above
Silvery wallpaper, mirrors and shimmering lights lend a glamorous touch

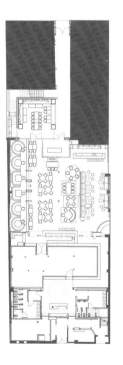

Left
Entering via the long breezeway and through the courtyard, the room has a lofty and open feel with two distinct spaces for dining and for lounging

Right
In the elevated dining area, large U-shaped banquettes offer the perfect perch to observe the scene

eat
Enjoy

Right
A cosy bar lounge provides a quiet
gathering place. Vibrant pink lighting
and the mirrored bar set the room
aglow

relax
Recharge

Toronto is a city bursting at the seams. It boasts, by attendance, the largest film festival in the world, a diverse multicultural population that speaks over 100 languages and dialects, is the starting point of the world's longest street, is home to the world's tallest freestanding structure, and the Hockey Hall of Fame. With over five million people living in the Greater Toronto area, it is no wonder that you sometimes crave an escape in the city.

Located on the shores of Lake Ontario, Toronto is Canada's leading business district and the country's largest city, and as such works hard and plays hard. The city is a confluence of green space, waterways and a unique system of natural ravines. Here, the city's residents can find an abundance of choice in their pursuit of rest and relaxation.

For the work weary, escape from the wheeling and dealing of the downtown core lies close at hand. Many restaurants and lounges can be found in the Distillery District, St Lawrence Market area, and the emerging restaurant row on King Street West. C Lounge, a club with a South Beach vibe, replete with swimming pool, private cabanas, and swaying palm trees, is a welcome oasis for the city's young professionals. Nearby Lux is retro cool and offers a new take on the 1970s bachelor pad.

relax Recharge

To the west, those same urbanites have descended upon the city's neglected areas on Queen Street to favour hip hangouts with an edge. In the historic Parkdale neighbourhood, the Drake Hotel is a beacon of upscale bohemian-chic. The transformation starts at the street edge, where the shiny black skin and 1940s-cool, chrome-lettered marquee sits in stark contrast to the orange neon sign flashing 'hotel' and rusticated cream faux-stone facade. Down the road, the Gladstone Hotel is more an exercise of discovery and restoration. Built in 1889 in the Richardsonian Romanesque style, the Gladstone is today home to 37 guest suites individualised by local artists, poets and designers, as well as art exhibit spaces, a performance venue, and the city's only functioning hand-operated lift. While locals may decry the gentrification of West Queen West, there is no doubt that these unique hotels have revitalised a strip of the city long forgotten.

Looking for retail therapy instead? The massive Eaton Centre, designed by renowned Canadian architect Eberhard Zeidler, lies at the commercial centre of Yonge Street and Dundas Street. Brand-conscious buyers will want to head to BMW Toronto – a stylised modern glass billboard in the east end of the city – or to the ritzy shops on Bloor Street in the north. Adjacent to the museum district, Bloor Street is the perfect spot to gaze at Daniel Libeskind's reworking of the Royal Ontario Museum or simply to people-watch on a summer day.

Those who prefer to relax outdoors will also find Toronto does not disappoint. A long, winding 43 kilometres (27 miles) of lakeshore outlines the city while a lengthy network of pathways snakes its way through the city's verdant ravines. Lined with bike paths, fragrant gardens, outdoor pavilions, waterside dining, and the glistening sky-lit buildings of the soon to be redeveloped Harbourfront area, the lakefront is a mecca for tourists

in the summertime. Across the water, the Toronto Islands are a staple for summer respite and a destination unto themselves. Accessible only by water taxi or ferry boat, the Islands offer everything from verdant green spaces for Frisbee games or romantic picnics for two, to wide paths for the city's many joggers, inline skaters and cyclists.

Demonstrating the social consciousness of Torontonians, there are venues to relax and recharge the mind as well as the body. The Sisterhood of St John the Divine Convent offers a place for solitary contemplation and retreat. Set in a wooded enclave in north Toronto, the convent is a light-filled, spacious building thoroughly modern in design. Plan a visit at dusk when the stained-glass windows of the chapel and towering clerestory radiate a heavenly amber glow from the religious services within, beckoning all to this sanctuary. In the same light, the new Bloorview Kids Rehab provides refuge to children with disabilities and their families. Set directly adjacent against a natural ravine, Bloorview is more a living, breathing entity than it is a hospital. With hands-on gardens and meandering pathways, it is full of life and vitality; this wonderful new home for Canada's largest paediatric rehabilitation facility is a testament to the extent to which the city cares for its young, its old, and everyone in between.

Bloorview Kids Rehab

Montgomery Sisam Architects / Stantec Architects

Leaside, north Toronto   2005

That hospitals are designed to be functional in treating illness is a basic expectation, but beyond quantitative issues of state-of-the-art equipment or floor area efficiencies the challenge for designers truly lies in addressing the qualitative aspects that promote patient well-being. It is well known by healthcare designers that the quality of a space has a profound impact on the healing process. With this in mind, a hospital should not be designed as a machine fed by sterile corridors but instead it should be interpreted as a verdant wetland; a living, breathing entity, full of life and vitality that has the spatial richness and cadence of the best communal environments.

Through what some critics have called the finest example of contemporary architecture in the city, the Bloorview Kids Rehab (originally the Bloorview MacMillan Children's Centre) makes a strong statement about the value of embracing change in the way healthcare spaces are conceived and considered. Designed by local architects Montgomery Sisam (of noted projects including the Humber River bicycle pedestrian bridge and the newly opened Toronto Botanical Gardens) in joint venture with Stantec, the hospital, in the broadest sense, addresses the physical but also the spiritual aspects of the healing process. Set on the edge of the vast Leaside Ravine in north Toronto, the hospital offers residents and their families a variety of therapeutic and social spaces including a gymnasium and pool, the Bloorview MacMillan School, a research library and a rehabilitation centre. The project also makes strong natural connections through a series of hands-on gardens and meandering pathways that tie into the adjacent ravine.

The therapeutic power of natural light and the access to nature was certainly not underestimated. On the outside of the wedge-shaped west wing, which rises like a natural hillside from two storeys to six, the designers created an earth-tone brick base and used a warm-grey zinc patterned to mimic weathered wooden shingles. As the zinc changes its patina with the weather, horizontal bands of coloured and clear glass provide a fanciful illuminated effect. Along its sloped edge, the metal roof cuts itself away to expose several spacious outdoor terraces. Anticipating light, rain and wind to penetrate through the filigree of wooden trellises and ivy, the terraces reinforce the concept of a hospital as a living building. Montgomery Sisam also placed group spaces and dining rooms adjacent to these outdoor terraces with the hope that indoor activities would spill outside on warm summer days. To further blur the distinction between inside and out, the project makes generous use of glass and natural materials such as warm cherry woods and soft limestone. Wood is

project

Bloorview Kids Rehab
25 Buchan Court, Leaside, Toronto, Ontario

architect
Montgomery Sisam Architects in joint venture with Stantec Architects

telephone
+1 416 425 6220

website
www.bloorviewmacmillan.on.ca

opening hours
not available

neighbourhood
Leaside, a traditional residential neighbourhood in north Toronto

style
standing on the edge of a ravine, earth-tone brick and warm grey zinc transform the hospital into a living building

clientele
Children with disabilities or special needs and their families

signature experience
watching the midday sun dance across amber-coloured glass louvres reflecting the etched poetic script onto the floor

other projects
Montgomery Sisam Architects: Toronto Botanical Garden, Toronto; Humber River Bicycle Pedestrian Bridge, Toronto
Stantec Architecture Ltd: 51 Division Police Station, Toronto

Opposite
Bloorview functions more like a community centre than a hospital, as the resource centre, pool and gymnasium are also open for use by local residents

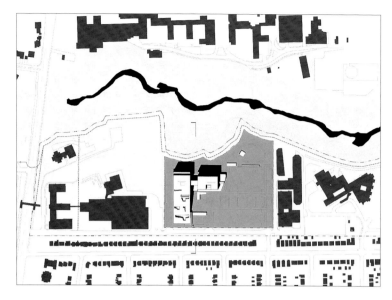

actually of great value in a hospital as it offers warmth and soft texture, but more importantly it responds to our inherent connections to nature. Balancing the rich woods is a carefully placed colour palette of rich plum, green apple, and ochre yellow accents.

In general, people need to have a sense of control over their environment and the freedom to explore. In the healthcare setting, this is particularly valuable in that it gives patients the sense of hope and opportunity as they battle with serious injury or life-long disability. Led by project partners Terry Montgomery and the late Christian Klemt, the design team intentionally positioned clusters of activity destinations alongside naturally lit pathways and glazed bridges that overlook natural gardens or green roof terraces – a far cry from the dark antiseptic corridors of early hospitals. The plantings and green roofs also support the hospital's desire to embrace a sustainable agenda and the architect's desire to create a retreat within the city.

The heart of the L-shaped scheme is the double-height family resource centre. Created as the place where the city and the ravine come together, the resource centre is a fluid and active space from which all other programmes radiate. With panoramic views of the adjacent ravine, visitors can congregate and get their bearings while those already familiar with the hospital can observe the comings and goings. Flooded with natural light, the low wooden ceiling and colourful splashes of green mosaic tile add a natural feel to the room. Interestingly, Bloorview functions more like a community centre than a hospital, as the resource centre, pool and gymnasium are also open for use by local residents. For children, this sense of connection with their normal rhythms rather than being insulated from the outside world is a vital aspect in their healing process as they often spend weeks, months and even years in treatment.

The benefits of art are also well considered. Rather than simply decorating the halls with animated characters or floral motifs, 'islands of interest' designed by local artists and the hands of the young patients themselves create an interactive and imaginative experience of light and touch. Expressing the themes of nature, transformation and history, the installations are intentionally abstract rather than literal. In the main lobby, artist Jan MacKie created *Whispered Invitation*, a curtain of over 5000 hand-formed coloured glass beads. Triggered by the motion of children, waves of colour wash across the beads and create a cosmological movement as the fluid patterns emulate the northern lights. In the glazed links that connect the building's east and west wings, artist Stuart Reid envisioned *To Cross this Passage*, a series of amber-coloured glass

louvres etched with a poetic script. As the sun traces its path, the halls become animated with the dance of golden light as the script is projected onto the floor below. Reid also adorned the entrance with *To Make this Voyage*, a canopy of similar amber glass panels etched with silhouettes of flying children. But the most emotional of all the installations is also the least technical. Created by children with disabilities, a tactile mosaic of hand-patterned ceramic tiles featuring elaborate birds or just simple dents and wiggles gives children an opportunity to make their own mark on their home away from home.

Below
A colour palette of rich plum, green
apple, and ochre yellow accents the
warm woods and soft limestone used
throughout the building

relax
Recharge

Left
Bloorview provides a number of
humanistic spaces for its patients
including hands-on gardens and
meandering pathways

Below
Diagram illustrating the relationship of
building pieces including low walls and
the sloping mass of the patient wing

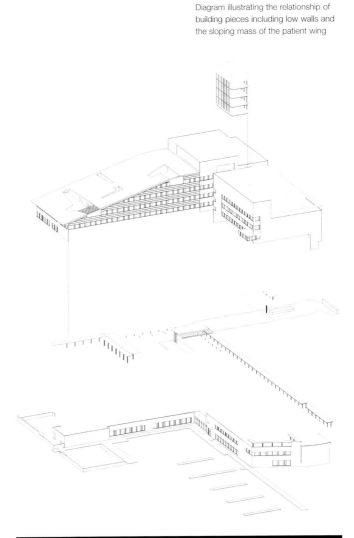

Above
Within the L-shaped plan, the family
resource centre and cafeteria are conceived as the place where the city
and the ravine come together, and the
point from which all other programmes
radiate

Right
Along the sloped edge, the metal roof
is cut away to expose outdoor terraces
on to which light, rain and wind are
allowed to penetrate through a filigree
of wooden trellises

Above
The hospital offers residents and their families a variety of therapeutic and social spaces including a gymnasium and pool, the Bloorview MacMillan School, a research library and a rehabilitation centre

Right
Group spaces and dining rooms sit adjacent to outdoor terraces with the hope that indoor activities may spill outside on warm summer days

relax
Recharge

Right
Bloorview functions more like a community centre than a hospital, as horizontal bands of coloured and clear glass provide a fanciful illuminated effect

Right
On the outside of the wedge-shaped west wing, the designers created an earth-tone brick base and used a warm-grey zinc patterned to mimic weathered wooden shingles

Left
Taking full advantage of its unique exposure to the highway, the building mixes sophistication and spectacle as passing motorists are tempted with titillating displays of new cars showcased four storeys above the street

Below
Whether looking down in anticipation piloting along the Don Valley Parkway or looking up in envy as you drive by the building exudes a sleek energy

BMW Toronto

Quadrangle Architects Ltd
Don Valley Parkway, Toronto   2003

Near the mouth of the Don River, where two major transport arteries converge, there is little to attract the attention of motorists passing at 120 kilometres per hour, save a few derelict industrial buildings and a highway on-ramp. Probably more interested in rushing to and from the city's core, few paid any attention when demolition began on an unused office building by the highway's edge. If anything, there might have felt a strange tinge of nostalgia for the old Lever Bros Sunlight Soap Company, a neighbourhood fixture – and source of soap smell – since the early 1970s. Yet, with only the concrete skeleton left exposed, a curious shift occurred as a fresh skin of glass began to wrap the massive six-storey hulk, forming what would eventually become the city's most spectacular urban billboard.

Designed by local firm Quadrangle Architects, BMW Toronto is the flagship retail showroom for a company that fully understands what gives this brand its cool-factor: the cars. Taking maximum advantage of its unique exposure to the highway, the building mixes sophistication and spectacle as passing motorists are tempted with titillating displays of new cars showcased four storeys above the street. Set three over two, the formal, white-framed display cases prompt passers-by to wonder if they are indeed real. And while the mass is clad in blue-tinted glass, the pillboxes feature an ultra-clear lead-free glass, evoking playful memories of the familiar matchbox car carrying case of our youth. From the inside, the cars are ghosted against a screen of frosted glass.

By day, the sober glass facade appears darkly translucent and quietly slips beyond the edges of the building. Reading more like a theatrical scrim hanging in mid air, its message is delivered partly by a massive three-storey backlit billboard clipped to the outer skin. At night, however, the glass wall disappears as the interior comes aglow, its full complement now becoming part of the spectacle.

Building up rather than out, the showrooms are spread vertically over five floors, with each one intentionally positioned and finished to deliver an exceptonal retail experience. In as much as BMW markets itself as the ultimate driving machine, this retailing *tour de force* has become the ultimate lifestyle machine, offering everything from cappuccinos to cabriolets while you take in the smell of premium leather and factory fresh air. On the ground floor, new models are set out in a loop, tracing an oval path directly past the adjacent 'lifestyle boutique' featuring all the style-minded accoutrements associated with BMW ownership, from hats to child-size roadsters.

Contrasted against the corporate mandated consistent palette of white and grey, the brightly coloured roadsters add yet another layer of drama to the already dynamic showroom space. Nearby, the fully exposed service bays are also celebrated and, as expected, are immaculate; the floors are implanted with thousands of small German clinker tiles that are

project
BMW Toronto
11 Sunlight Park Road, Toronto, Ontario

architect
Quadrangle Architects Ltd

telephone
+1 416 623 4269

website
www.bmwtoronto.ca

opening hours
Mon – Thurs: 9am to 8pm
Fri – Sat: 9am to 6pm

neighbourhood
at the crossroads of the Don Valley Parkway and Gardiner Expressway, the two main thoroughfares into the downtown Toronto core

style
a sober glass facade punctuated by an ever-changing six car 'living billboard'

clientele
BMW and Mini enthusiasts ogling the latest roadster while sifting through accessories in the Lifestyle Boutique

signature experience
waiting in the top floor 'vehicle delivery lounge' as your new BMW emerges from the brightly polished stainless-steel freight lift

other projects
Candy Factory Lofts, Toronto; The CHUM Building, Toronto

Left
The showrooms are spread vertically over five floors, with each one intentionally positioned and finished to deliver a unique retail experience

Below
Near the mouth of the Don River, where two major transport arteries converge, there is little else to attract the attention of motorists passing at 120 kph

Above
By day, the sober glass facade appears darkly translucent and quietly slips beyond the edges of the building

impervious to oil stains. Looking on from the mezzanine level, from where you can watch the choreographed actions of precision German engineers, the luxurious customer lounge is outfitted with chic black leather club loungers, plasma televisions, a cappuccino bar, and individual workstations with Aeron chairs fully hot-wired for the internet. You move up to the lounge by calling for the exquisitely formal glass lift or taking the encircling open granite and steel stairs. Floor three is dedicated to the fast lane, featuring motorcycles and the high performance M-series, while the fourth caters to previously enjoyed vehicles.

But the dramatic final act is saved for those able to reach the top. Emerging from one of two brightly polished stainless-steel freight lifts, their new toys are introduced to the owners in the vehicle delivery lounge; a fantastic double-height space on the west corner, designed appropriately with panoramic views of the financial core across the river. Whether looking down in anticipation of piloting along the Don Valley Parkway, or looking up in envy as you drive by, the lounge exudes a sleek energy, exactly what one would expect from a premium brand. And if this is not enough, the showroom space can host social events for up to 300 guests.

In what is clearly a market aimed at a fast-paced, urban car culture, the project also maintains some very high environmental standards. As the brownfield site is prone to flooding, the designers incorporated verdant drainage swales to purify the stormwater before returning it to the river. Working with the Task Force to Bring Back the Don and the Toronto Region Conservation Authority, a system of downlighting keeps excessive night glare to a minimum, while a computerised system of light dimming keeps migratory birds away. A regular participant in Doors Open Toronto, BMW Toronto's crown jewel-box has won several architectural and urban design awards and is rightfully regarded as one of Toronto's marquee buildings.

Opposite
Contrasted against the consistent palette of white and grey, the brightly coloured roadsters add yet another layer of drama to the already dynamic showroom space

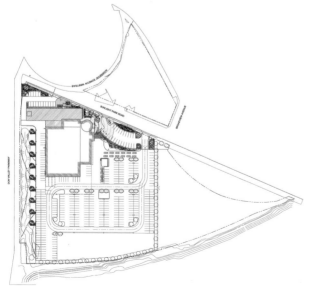

Above
At night, the glass wall disappears
as the interior comes aglow, its full
complement now becoming part of
the spectacle

Left
BMW Toronto is located near the mouth
of the Don River, where, save for a few
derelict industrial buildings, little else
memorable exists

relax
Recharge

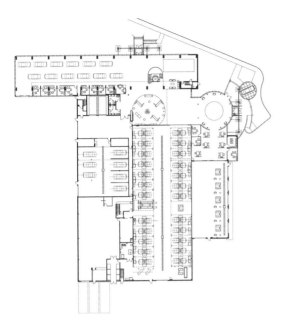

Above
Building up rather than out, the showrooms are spread vertically over five
floors. On the ground floor, new models
are set out in a loop, tracing an oval
path directly past the adjacent lifestyle
boutique

Below
On the north elevation, the architects
inserted the city's largest interactive
billboard.

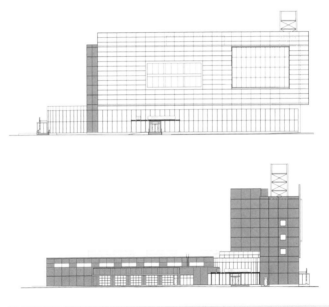

Right
A fresh skin of glass wraps the massive
six-storey hulk, forming what has
become the city's most spectacular
urban billboard

BMW Toronto

Left
On the ground floor, new models are set out in a loop, tracing an oval path directly past the adjacent 'lifestyle boutique' featuring all the style-minded accoutrements associated with BMW ownership – from hats to child-size roadsters

Below
Cars are ghosted against a screen of frosted glass in the main showroom *(bottom)* on the ground floor, while level three *(below)* is dedicated to the fast lane, featuring motorcycles and the high performance M-series

C Lounge

Nicholas Mazilu, Rapt Digital Design Labs

Wellington Street West, Toronto   2006

project
C Lounge
456 Wellington Street West, Toronto,
Ontario

architect
Nicholas Mazilu, Rapt Digital Design
Labs

telephone
+1 416 260 9393

website
www.libertygroup.com/c_lounge/
c_lounge.html

opening hours
Mon: 10pm to close
Thurs: 5pm to 9pm
Fri: 9.30pm to close
Sat: 10pm to close

neighbourhood
nestled between nondescript factories
just south of the King West village

style
a sexy spa-inspired bar, with slick
leather sofas and a rooftop pool
surrounded by private VIP cabanas

clientele
Toronto hipsters, visiting celebrities, and
the downtown work crowd

signature experience
schmoozing and socialising at 'After
Work Thursdays'

other projects
Wild Indigo Martini Bar, Toronto

Like so many of the other commercial streets in the area, Wellington is typical by all rights; a functional nondescript stretch of semi-industrial brick buildings that becomes a virtual ghost town by dusk. Offering little in the way of a contemporary urban experience, it's hard to imagine that a trendy lounge would see any reason to set up shop here. But this is the perfect location for a place that aims to carry the work-weary crowd away from the daily woes of being the urban working young.

By far the city's most sultry urban oasis, C Lounge is an intoxicating mix of nightclub and spa that is perhaps more South Beach than it is Toronto. Owner Nick Di Donato (also of Liberty Grand and Rosewater Supper club fame) and architectural designer Nicholas Mazilu at Rapt Digital Design Labs have created a stylish chameleon that transforms itself literally with each season.

Inside, the long and narrow space is simple and to the point. Travertine flooring, beige walls and rich soothing brown leather are the standard. On one side, the bar is clearly the focal point of the room as three pendant lights cast a warm down-glow across the solid black granite top and rich cherry-wood face. Behind the bar a blood-red wall sparkles from the white light of thirty crystalline light fixtures. On the opposite wall, cascading sheer curtains divide the room into a string of intimate, alluring lounge areas accentuated by warm leather sectionals, soothing burgundy ottomans and dark mahogany tables.

But what is more intoxicating about the space is not necessarily what you see but how it is revealed. Gypsy Rose Lee used the power of visual temptation to popularise striptease in the 1930s, and it is this same notion that permeates the design of C Lounge. Our internal voyeur knows all too well that the beauty of seduction lies less in the revealed than in the act of revealing. Akin to an erotic piece of lingerie, the translucent cascading veils do as much to conceal and then skilfully expose, as they do to define the lounge spaces. As you move from front to back, the veil is actually a device for sensory temptation, providing an enticing and suggestive glimpse of who resides within. Lit by a single overhead pendant and candlelight, the radiant glow emanating from its textured surfaces intentionally teases the senses and creates a state of excited anticipation as the magic unfolds before our eyes.

As you participate in the experience – for to simply say 'enter' is a gross misrepresentation – you are simultaneously transformed into an observer and an event. Teasing out the shy inner voyeur yet again, the luxurious communal powder room doubles as a protective cocoon where inhibitions can be shed in any one of the purposely designed, gender

Right
As seductive as a piece of lingerie, the translucent cascading veils do as much to conceal and then skilfully expose, as they do to define the lounge spaces

relax *Recharge*

Right
The bar is clearly the focal point of the room as three pendant lights cast a warm down-glow across the solid black granite top and rich cherry-wood face

Right
The luxurious communal powder
room doubles as a protective cocoon
where inhibitions can be shed in any
one of the purposely designed gender-
ambiguous cubicles

Below
Patrons can move past the textured
glass to the outdoor lounge, replete
with glowing pool and VIP cabanas

Above
Cascading sheer curtains divide the
room into a string of intimate, alluring
lounge areas accentuated by warm
leather sectionals, soothing burgundy
ottomans and dark mahogany tables

Opposite
C Lounge is an intoxicating mix of
nightclub and spa that is perhaps more
South Beach than it is Toronto

ambiguous cubicles. But unwilling to simply limit us to the role of observer,
Di Donato grants us the joy of interactive participation as any number of
personal finishing touches can be had, including hair and make-up touch-
ups along with full massage services by professionally trained Aveda
specialists.

Armed with restored red lipstick or a cologne refresher, patrons can
move past the textured glass to the outdoor lounge to test out their newly
acquired fantasies by the poolside. Under the faint moonlight, the verdant
patio is an intimate spa-like experience as the flicker of candlelight dances
across the smooth surface of the glowing turquoise pool. Along the outer
edge, personal VIP cabanas and low-slung bamboo loungers are set deep
behind a veil of ecru canvas curtains while ambient music confirms what
we already know. Here things are whispered and quiet. Here things are
most profound. Here anything can happen.

Sitting in a white leather chaise longue, it's not hard to forget that C
Lounge is in Toronto, a seasonal home to the winter blues. No problem.
With the help of a 185-square-metre (220 square yards) insulated tent, the
patio transforms itself into C Lounge's baby brother – Toronto's first ICE
Lounge. Designed by Heidi Bayley of Iceculture, curtains of crystal clear
ice surround an oversized frozen bar flanked by ice couches, tables and
chairs, and of course, ice tumblers filled with the popular mojito cocktail.
And what was once the pool is transformed into a sunken seating area
with a large abstract ice sculpture in the middle. Of course, the fashion-
conscious are treated to custom-designed parkas as they chill to new
lows in their unique urban ice experience.

The Drake Hotel

3rd UNCLE design inc
Queen Street West, Toronto   2004

project
The Drake Hotel
1150 Queen Street West, Toronto,
Ontario

architect
3rd UNCLE design inc

telephone
+1 416 531 5042

website
www.thedrakehotel.ca

opening hours
Mon – Sun: all hours

neighbourhood
in the booming west Queen Street West
district, the artistic and design hub of
the city

style
a blend of eclectic materials, hip
modern design, and art-house chic
raise the appeal of this funkified former
flophouse

clientele
unpretentious and welcoming, the
hotel is a playground for Queen Street
denizens and the hipsterati alike

signature experience
enjoying the tunes of local undiscovered
talent in the cosy, recreation room-like
Underground venue downstairs

other projects
Shanghai Cowgirl, Toronto; Lileo,
Toronto

Replete with a mixed bag of everything from flophouses for the less fortunate to trendy galleries for the artistic-at-heart, there is no denying the fact that Parkdale, also known as the Queen West art and design district, is the quintessential gritty urban neighbourhood. Parkdale was once one of the city's wealthiest neighbourhoods, yet decades of neglect have left an aged patina on the fabric and the faces of its residents. And while it is experiencing rapid gentrification (in the eyes of some it is merely a rediscovery), this is exactly the way Jeff Stober – internet trailblazer and the street's newest patron of cool – wants it, as his recent conversion of the Drake Hotel has made an indelible mark on the neighbourhood as the epitome of upscale bohemian-chic.

Originally known as Small's Hotel, a Canadian Pacific Railway hostelry on the fringes of town and then later renamed The Drake in 1949, the new Drake is indeed improved, but by no means is it your typical designer boutique hotel. Investing over CA$ 6 million and two years of his life, Stober was set on his mission to convert the dilapidated 110-year-old flophouse/punk bar into a grand salon-inspired nexus of style. To help make this vision a reality, Stober hired local architects 3rd UNCLE design, the conceptual design troupe known for serving up a collage of intellectual-kitsch inspired by found objects and funky urban artifacts. With a slightly bipolar slant, 'reduce, re-use, recycle' is more than a popular maxim, it is their working mantra. A perfect fit for the often unorthodox Parkdale arts scene.

The Drake is not the only old new kid on the block to experience a radical facelift. Just a few doors down is the Gladstone Hotel, another vintage brick and stone inn from the late 1800s recently restored by the Zeidler family, long-standing architectural fixtures in their own right. But while the Gladstone makes great strides to faithfully service the entrenched indigenous art crowd, the Drake represents a philosophically opposite strategy, choosing instead to cater to the bourgeois, urban up-and-comers. It is a strategy that seems to have worked as the hotel is fast becoming one of the city's most talked about social and overnight venues.

To service its post-modern grunge patrons, the hotel is an all-in-one venue; 19 guest suites – or crash pads – have been updated in a variety of finishes and themes, as has the bar/lounge, dining room and café, the yoga studio, the Underground music hall and the licensed outdoor rooftop patio, aka 'The Sky Yard'. The first real indications though of the uber-hip happenings within are actually visible from the street, as the shiny black skin and 1940s-cool, chrome-lettered marquee sits in stark contrast to the orange neon sign flashing 'hotel' and rusticated cream faux-stone facade. Step into the lobby, however, and the full effect of 3rd UNCLE's manic vision immediately takes hold.

No linear description can do this space justice – it is quite simply a haphazard collage of disparate elements from just about anything that 3rd

Right
Not taking itself too seriously, the boutique hotel features many whimsical details

Below
The main social space is a loft-inspired playpen where lounge, bar and dining room converge into one another

The Drake Hotel

relax
Recharge

Right
Designed by local architects 3rd UNCLE
design, the dining room is an exercise in
sumptuous retro-chic and an antidote
to crisp modern design so prevalent in
clubs and lounges

UNCLE could cobble together. But make no mistake, what seems like a schizophrenic mélange of found objects, is actually an intentional exercise in retro-chic aesthetic; precisely the reason the Drake fits in so well here. No one asks why there is a pommel horse in the lobby or paper bag light fixtures, they are just accepted, but then again so too are the chalk board walls covered in daily graffiti and a colourful chandelier fabricated from stripped out bicycle frames. Seeing themselves as patently authentic representing the true character of the street, the sense that this is unmistakably an antidote to the crisp modern design so prevalent in the clubs and lounges of the late 1990s is obvious.

The main social space is a loft-inspired playpen where lounge, bar and dining room converge into one another. With Rorschach flocked wallcoverings and clear plastic ottomans with exposed springs, it's easy to become immersed in the urban fantasy, yet peel back the layers and some of the original 1930s details, such as banisters and wainscoting, can still be found. But exploration is exactly the point, as 3rd UNCLE has creatively imparted new interpretations and future uses into almost every detail, not all that dissimilar to the neighbourhood itself. As a contrast to all this drama, the designers also recognised the need for creature comforts in the guest suites. Designed to suit varying degrees of needs, vintage furniture is offset with glass tile and LCD monitors. Not taking itself too seriously though, the hotel has recently introduced a series of racy accessories to its room service menu.

Although there is no real model for anything like this, Stober cites as inspiration everything from the laid-back lounges of New York's Chelsea district in the 1930s, to David Brooks' *Bobos in Paradise* in which the bohemian bourgeois (yuppie descendants) revel in their expensive exotic purchases. Ironically, 3rd UNCLE's muse was a little more pragmatic; they conducted a photomontage of the neighbourhood to grasp the area's subtleties and then created a manuscript titled *Undersigning,* which is on display in the lobby.

What would a day at the Drake be like? Start with morning yoga followed by a long coffee in the café. Take a walk along Queen West past the appliance shops and a few art galleries, making it back in time for foie gras served with a pungent blackcurrant tea. A quick starter at the bar, an indie band in the Underground and then retire quietly to your room to check your emails. Strange bedfellows indeed, but this is exactly what makes the Drake a vital element in helping forge Toronto as a *Design City*; it is a hotel-cum-cultural community centre where art, music and food cohabit while quietly revelling in its unconventionality.

Above
Chalk board walls covered in daily
graffiti hang over the well stocked bar

Opposite
Offsetting the Rorschach flocked wallcoverings and clear plastic ottomans
with exposed springs lie some of the
original 1930s details, such as banisters
and wainscoting

Above
Suites feature vintage furniture offset with glass tile and LCD monitors catering to the needs of the urban clientele

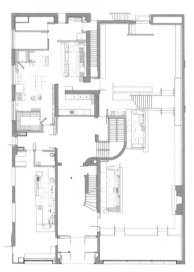

Above
From the main lobby the full effect of 3rd UNCLE's manic vision immediately takes hold. The principal social space is an open playpen where lounge, bar and dining room all cohabit

Right
To service its post-modern grunge patrons, the hotel is an all-in-one venue; 19 guest suites – or crash pads – have been updated in a variety of finishes and themes

Right
Reflecting the unique character of the
neighbourhood and the hotel's patrons,
the Drake offers up playful amenities –
including a Sky Yard and the Yoga Den

Gladstone Hotel

Zeidler Partnership Architects
Queen Street West, Toronto   2005

project
Gladstone Hotel
1214 Queen Street West, Toronto,
Ontario

architect
Zeidler Partnership Architects

telephone
+1 416 531 4635

website
www.gladstonehotel.com

opening hours
Mon – Sun: all hours

neighbourhood
an anchor in the Parkdale neighbourhood, where unconventional theatre
and indie art parties are the norm

style
restored Victorian grandeur punctuated
by sophisticated modern but eclectic
interiors

clientele
Parkdale old-timers, the artsy crowd,
and generation Y'ers in search of the
latest hip hangout

signature experience
ride the city's only functioning hand-
operated lift, while operator Hank regales
you with the tale of its discovery and
restoration

other projects
Toronto Eaton Centre, Toronto; Queen's
Quay Terminal, Toronto; Pan Pacific
Hotel, Vancouver

For those who believe the process of gentrification has a uniform negative impact on the social fabric of existing urban neighbourhoods, they obviously have not been recently to the Gladstone Hotel in the city's west end Parkdale neighbourhood. Restoring both the original Victorian grandeur and yet maintaining the urban grit that gives Parkdale its charm, the once dilapidated flophouse proves that gentrification does not always mean the indiscriminate displacement of indigenous culture with yuppie cafés and chic lounges.

Originally built in 1889 in the Richardsonian Romanesque style, the Gladstone is the oldest continuously operating hotel in Toronto and has always had a strong connection with the surrounding neighbourhood. While the original ornate cupola and ironwork were removed in the late 1930s, much of the original brick, arched-window millwork, rough-cut stone and gargoyles remain intact. Even before the restoration, the hotel had a wonderful street presence given its original history as a stylish hostelry for commercial travellers disembarking at the now-demolished Parkdale railway station.

Recently a respite for many a lost soul, today it is the home of 37 guest suites individualised by local artists, poets, and designers, as well as art exhibit spaces, a performance venue and, of course, the original lounge still frequented daily by old-timers. Interestingly, it is also home to the city's only functioning hand-operated lift; the tale of its discovery and restoration is gladly recounted by Hank, its resident operator.

Seeing the value buried underneath years of neglect, the project is the brainchild of local artist and filmmaker Christina Zeidler, daughter of the famed Toronto architect Eberhard Zeidler (of Eaton Centre and Ontario Place fame). Taking their cues from the writings of urban theorist and personal friend, the late Jane Jacobs, who explained in her seminal text *The Death and Life of Great American Cities* that new ideas must use old buildings,[1] the Gladstone is less about commercialising history as it is an ideological experiment in democratic community enhancement. So, rather than displacing the pack of regulars with the well-heeled SUV elite looking for Philippe Starck fixtures and pretentious minimalism, the hotel recycles many of its original social collision points and offers them back into the public realm as spaces to interact, to experience art, community and culture for a variety of users; a perfect backdrop to an already lively and diverse community art scene.

At the ground level much of the original albeit slightly ramshackle charm has been retained. Greeting visitors is the grand red brick lobby

Right
Recently a respite for many a lost soul, today the Gladstone is home to 37 guest suites individual-ised by local artists, poets and designers, as well as art exhibit spaces, a performance venue, and the original lounge still frequented daily by old-timers

relax *Recharge*

Right
Originally built in 1889 in the Richardsonian Romanesque style, the Gladstone is the oldest continuously operating hotel in Toronto

with its golden hardwood floors and massive creaky wooden staircase. Beside, the long and narrow Art Bar and Ballroom with its sunken chairs and arched corner windows is a quieter alternative to the adjacent and often raucous Melody Bar, offering decorative column capitals, ornate plaster friezes and some of the wildest Karaoke in the city.

The most creative example of Christina's ideological makeover, however, is the guest suites on the upper floors. Here, sameness is gladly

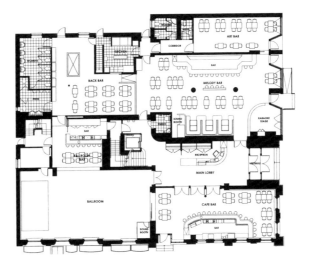

Right
Much of the original layout has been
preserved and restored. The hotel
recycles many of its original social
collision points including the long and
narrow Art Bar and the adjacent, and
often raucous, Melody Bar

passed over in favour of originality, as each suite is themed entirely on the free creativity of their individual designers. Before you even enter the rooms, the generous 2.75-metre (9 feet) wide corridors and large open foyers, with their old and creaky hardwood floors, double as gallery spaces for artists, some of whom have become permanent residents. And while some of the furniture has been upgraded, it is still unpretentious; indeed, a few of the hotel's original armchairs with the letter 'G' carved into the back can still be found.

Depending on your fancy, the guest rooms range from sophisticated and elegant to complete kitsch. Room 404 *Canadiana*, by Jenny Francis, Charlene Gilmour, and Grant Gilmour plays homage to the north with warm cedar panelling, a full-size mural of a forest and a mock moose antler chandelier painted white. For Kathryn Walter and Room 416, felt was the material of choice as everything from the furniture to the lampshades to the semi-spherical orbs that cover the walls is a testament to the versatility and romance of the material. *The Blue Line Room*, by former Bruce Mau design associate Barr Gilmore and interior designer Michel Arcand, is a combination of contemporary graphic, furniture and media design. Painted entirely in Chroma-Key blue, the room allows visitors to make their own digital videos and insert their choice of backdrop later. Adding to the sexiness of the room, contemporary furniture pieces include a Periphere Uno lounge chair and two Kartell Bourgie table lamps. If you prefer something a little more retro, *Lehtinen Lodge* evokes nostalgia for Canada's resort history with 1930s modernism combined with rich wood tones and a central fireplace. And finally, in the tower on the south-west corner, a deluxe two-storey suite has been designed by Christina herself for larger groups and special events. It's nothing short of spectacular with the second-floor loft bedroom having 360 degree panoramic views of the city and Lake Ontario.

Whether you are a guest spending a few nights, or simply stopping by for an afternoon drink, you very quickly appreciate the deeply felt connection this iconic place has in the consciousness of the neighbourhood. Granted, the Gladstone is not your typical boutique hotel, but then again, neither is Parkdale your typical neighbourhood, where unconventional theatre and indie art parties are the norm. Like the community that supports its artists, the Gladstone is exactly what it wants and needs to be: a backdrop allowing ideas to happen.

Above
The *Blue Line Room* is a combination
of graphics, furniture and media design,
and features contemporary furniture
pieces including a Periphere Uno lounge
chair and Kartell Bourgie table lamps

Opposite
Clean lines and a crisp palette define
the *Offset Room*

1   Jane Jacobs. *The Death and Life of Great American Cities*, Random House,
    New York, 1961

Right
The tower on the south-west corner features a deluxe two-storey suite with panoramic views of the city

Lux

munge//leung: design associates

King Street West, Toronto   2004

project
Lux
720 King Street West, Toronto, Ontario

architect
munge//leung: design associates

telephone
+1 416 203 2883

website
www.luxonking.com

opening hours
Mon – Sun: 4 pm to 1 am

neighbourhood
in the trendy King Street West restaurant and club district

style
chic and intimate retro style lounge/ restaurant with mid-twentieth-century modern furnishings, marble tabletops, mirror and chrome accents

clientele
young and stylish Toronto hipsters

signature experience
relaxing in your Barcelona chair, martini in hand, enjoying the sounds of Tom Jones drifting in the background

other projects
This Is London, Toronto ; Dragonfly Nightclub, Fallsview Casino Resort, Niagara Falls

Over the years, Toronto has indeed seen its fair share of trendy restaurants and food fads come and go. In the 1980s it was modern Italian packaged with a glamorous urban glitz. The 1990s saw star chefs eschew formal eateries in favour of smaller bistros, even moving into what could only be termed 'farm chic', when famed chef Michael Stadtlander started hosting agrarian summer picnics at his Singhampton farm. Today, the rage among hip foodies is the Supper Club, an eclectic marriage of high quality restaurant with the urban lounge.

No longer pining for uber-hip boutiques serving up fad fare with a dose of attitude, Toronto's moneyed class have style, taste and experience, and with it are looking for a seamless transition from after-work cocktails to full-on gastronomic delights, continuing the party well into the evening. Leading the pack in reshaping our expectations about entertainment is nightlife kingpin Charles Khabouth, also of Ultra Supper Club fame, Pantages Hotel, and Guvernment, the popular clubland megaplex.

His latest offering is Lux, a contemporary reinterpretation of the quintessential 1970s bachelor pad in the hip King Street West restaurant district. Not all that dissimilar to the design sensibility of the city itself, Lux embraces timeless design and historical moments and assimilates them together with a palette of ultra-modern and retro-cool to titillate the senses, grant moments of casual intimacy and create a mosaic full of movement and depth.

Like a modern-day *flâneur*, dining – or rather participating – at Lux is all about seeing and being seen. From the obese orange lettering stencilled on the windows, through to the bar on the back wall with a full panoramic view, the space is designed to permit maximum gazing from all points within. Starting in the lounge, the space oozes a metallic sheen, enhanced by a marriage of leather, smoked mirrors and plenty of chrome. Black leather Mies Barcelonas, ottomans and marble pavilion tables share the space with white pony-haired chairs and set themselves up around a lavish Mare Black travertine and wooden fireplace. Hanging overhead, organic tendrils in charcoal hues add a delicate layer of filigree, while hand-printed wallpaper decorates the back wall.

Reflected in the lounge's full-height mirrored wall, the light-coloured bar with its opulent Azul Macaubas granite top shines within the room. A string of mirror balls by designer Tom Dixon floats overhead while a full-height wine rack inset with horizontal strings of mirror adds colour and sparkle. Catching the eye at the end of the bar, a column of framed postcards set the colour palette for the dining room. If the lounge is too

Right
From the obese orange lettering stencilled on the windows, through to the bar on the back wall with a full panoramic view, the space is designed to permit maximum gazing from all points within

relax
Recharge

Right
Lux claims its territory along the hip
King Street West restaurant district

Left
With a series of zones, Lux offers a seamless transition from after-work cocktails to full-on gastronomic delights, continuing the party well into the evening

Below
Black leather *Barcelona* chairs and ottomans and marble pavilion tables define the lounge area

pretentious, the dining area is certainly more welcoming, furnished entirely with mid-twentieth-century modern Eero Saarinen pedestal dining tables, swivelling fibre-glass Tulip chairs and tufted chartreuse banquettes. Adding a veil of softness, green sheer curtains offset the lime green banquettes and can be drawn to divide the space for private gatherings. Around the perimeter, red astro-shaped pendants add a splash of colour and evoke the ambience of a nostalgic, if not humorous, Jetson-esque folly.

Of course, the story of Lux is not just about serving up great design – it does serve food as well. Chef Jonathon Lucas has crafted a menu of urban comfort food that includes stone-baked tuna sashimi pizza, lobster ravioli in vanilla butter sauce, and organic Irish salmon. Not forgetting the clubland clientele, the bar features designer ice-cubes from Japan. While the house can seat up to 150 patrons, if so desired, the cost to rent the room starts at CA$500 a night.

Helping to steer this grand revisioning are local interior design talents Alessandro Munge and Sai Leung who, after first cutting their teeth at famed interior design studio Yabu Pushelburg, have gone on to develop a solid portfolio and reputation of their own as the most in-demand restaurant and nightclub design firm in the city. Having worked with Khabouth for many years, the creative dynamic trio is currently working on the Dragonfly Nightclub, a wonderful entertainment venue located in the Fallsview Casino Resort in Southern Ontario's Garden City of Niagara Falls, Canada.

Left
The lounge oozes a metallic sheen,
enhanced by a marriage of leather,
smoked mirrors and plenty of chrome

Below
White pony-haired chairs sit alongside
a lavish Mare Black travertine fireplace
finished in cowhide trim

Left
Hanging overhead, organic tendrils in
charcoal hues add a delicate filigree,
while hand-printed wallpaper decorates
the back wall

Left
A montage of framed postcards catches
the eye at the end of the bar

relax
Recharge

Right
The light-coloured bar with its opulent
Azul Macaubas granite top separates
the cosy lounge space from the dining
area

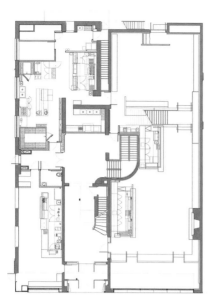

Above
Inside, the space is designed to permit maximum gazing, particularly from the main bar which overlooks the dining area

Right
The dining area is furnished with tufted chartreuse banquettes, Eero Saarinen pedestal dining tables and swivelling Tulip chairs, while sheer curtains that can be drawn to divide the space for private gatherings add a veil of softness

relax
Recharge

Convent for the Sisterhood of St Joh

Montgomery Sisam Architects Inc
Cummer Avenue, north Toronto   2006

project
Convent for the Sisterhood of St John the Divine
233 Cummer Avenue, Toronto, Ontario

architect
Montgomery Sisam Architects Inc

telephone
+1 416 531 5042

website
www.ssjd.ca/convent.html

opening hours
not available

neighbourhood
in a wooded enclave in a residential area of north Toronto

style
contemporary yet austere, filled with a blend of modern materials and ancient stained glass

clientele
home to the Sisters of St John the Divine, an Anglican order founded in 1884

signature experience
sitting in the chapel as the northern light strikes the soaring angular beech wall and fills the room with a heavenly glow

other projects
Bird Studies Canada Headquarters, Port Rowan, Ontario; Arts and Administration Building, University of Toronto, Scarborough Campus, Scarborough

When you think of a convent, the picture of an aged building, quiet and simple, set among verdant trees away from the bustle of modern life comes to mind. For the Sisterhood of St John the Divine, the desire to build a new home suited to meet the needs of a growing ministry and increased numbers of guests on retreat, resulted in something quite different: a light-filled, spacious building thoroughly modern in design. Contemporary and austere, it is a sanctuary in the city.

An Anglican order founded in 1884, the Sisterhood of St John the Divine has had only three homes in Toronto. With its last convent located in the north end of the city only metres from the 16-lane Highway 401, quiet contemplation and serene meditation were perhaps not easily achieved. For a new home, the sisters looked to a wooded enclave in North York on a patch of land beside St John's Rehab Hospital (currently undergoing its own renovation and expansion by Montgomery Sisam and Farrow Partnership Architects). The hospital was founded by the Sisterhood in 1937 and is still surrounded by a ring of trees planted by the sisters some 60 years ago.

Set well back from busy Cummer Avenue, the building is restrained and fits in with the natural setting. The complex consists of a simple two-storey brick building set in a figure of eight pattern, enclosing two private courtyards and incorporating a former nurses' residence which has been turned into a guest house. Save for the chapel, which extends outward and upward from the front lobby, the exterior is relatively unassuming with the length of pinkish brick interrupted only by random vertical windows. The stained-glass windows of the chapel – inherited from the previous convent – and towering clerestory remain unnoticeable until evening when light from the religious services within casts an ethereal, heavenly glow, beckoning all to this refuge.

A bowed timber-frame canopy set on slender metal pin legs marks the entry to the building. As you would expect, the convent is simple and modest. A grey speckled linoleum floor runs throughout, allowing some of the less mobile sisters and those resident in the infirmary to get about in their wheelchairs with ease. Use of sturdy oak for all the doors, the built-in furniture and freestanding cabinetry unifies the spaces. With a mission dedicated to both prayer and active ministry, the convent needed to accommodate both resident nuns and visitors alike. The shared spaces – the chapel, refectory, and community room – are clustered near the front of the building and are accessible to all. As in medieval monasteries, the residential areas for the sisters and the guest quarters are more private and organised in separate cloisters.

Extending from the lobby is a long corridor leading to the guest rooms, kept bright by the extensive glazing which allows sunlight to spill in from the interior courtyard. Across the hall, various meeting rooms, a servery and the library can be found. The library is a cosy and comfortable

e Divine

Below
A bowed timber-frame canopy set on slender metal pin legs marks the entry to the building.

Right
A series of stained-glass panels in the foyer are set aglow by the late afternoon sun

Left
Residents can enjoy quiet, contemplative moments while ensconced in their tiny private rooms, or outdoors in the private courtyards, where the extensive glazing allows light to spill into the interior

Left
The minimal design of the room provides the perfect backdrop to the sound of the pipe organ and voices raised in prayer, echoing against the vaulted ceiling

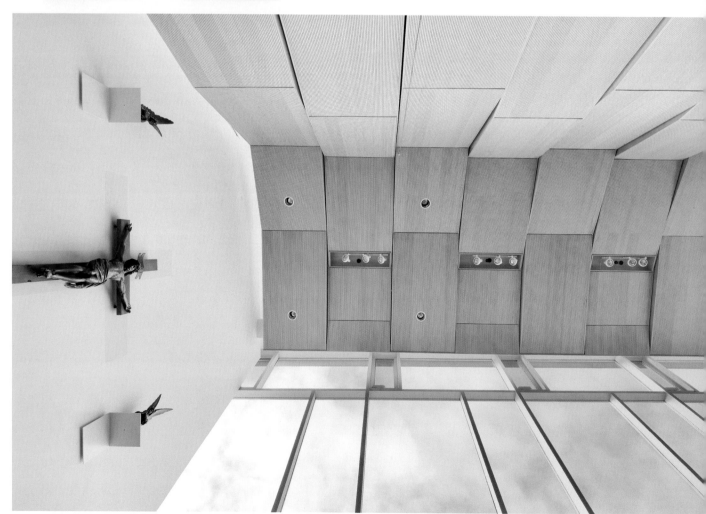

relax *Recharge*

Right
Save for the chapel which extends outward and upward from the front lobby,
the exterior is relatively unassuming as
the pinkish brick is interrupted only by
random vertical windows

Above
Chapel Ceiling: Detail of the beech ceiling in the chapel as its angular yet fluid
form folds upwards and overhead

Opposite
The most striking feature of the chapel
is the abundance of light and volume. A
soaring weave of beech ceiling panels,
angular yet fluid, stretches upwards and
overhead

space, with deep leather chairs for lounging and thousands of books on spiritual subjects to peruse. The same grainy oak has been used for the door and trim, the Librarian's desk, the library stacks, the study carrels, and even the traditional hanging card catalogue containing index cards ordered by the Dewey Decimal System. Down the hallway you enter the oldest part of the campus, the former nursing residence turned guest quarters. Residents can enjoy quiet, contemplative moments, either ensconced in their tiny private rooms or outdoors pondering the intricate stone labyrinth on the grounds. With air conditioning provided naturally using a sophisticated ventilation system and windows that open to the outside, this wing of the building with its small rooms and low ceilings is remarkably cool and comfortable.

The chapel is the true heart of the building and the sisters' spiritual life. Entry is through a massive swinging oak door into an anteroom. An ornate limestone mantel, formerly situated in the Reverend Sister's office at the last location, anchors the back wall. The grey linoleum transforms into a dove grey porcelain tile throughout the chapel, again allowing the space to be fully wheelchair accessible. Huge sliding oak doors set into a deep wooden frame mark the entrance into the main room.

The most striking feature of the chapel is the abundance of light and volume. A soaring weave of beech ceiling panels, angular yet fluid, stretches upwards and overhead. Suggestive of the protective hand of God, the interior skin provides a sense of safety to the sisters who sit and worship in the rows of pews beneath. Clerestory windows opposite bring the northern light in, opening the room to the heavens. At the end of the room stands the altar, solid and strong, carved out of limestone and featuring an eagle (the symbol of St John) and her eaglets on the facade, while the crucifix hangs behind, against a softly polished wall of Venetian plaster. The minimal design of the room provides the perfect backdrop to the sound of the pipe organ and voices raised in prayer, echoing against the vaulted ceiling.

Tucked behind the chapel, through a sandblasted glass door, is a small jewel of a room. Like the rest of the chapel, the room is spare and clean with white walls and little furniture. Yet the room glistens as opalescent glass tiles have been painstakingly set on the ceiling. The hues of the tiles mimic the hues in the single huge arched stained-glass window facing the street, which depicts a scene of St John walking with Mary after the crucifixion of Jesus. The window is over 100 years old and has graced each of the order's previous convents. Here is a perfect blend of old and new.

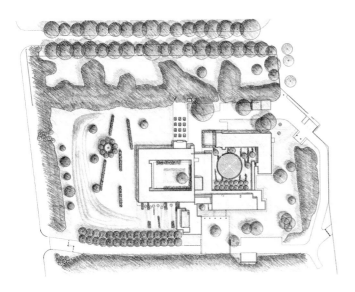

Left
For their new site, the Sisterhood looked to a wooded enclave in North York on a patch of land beside St John's Rehab Hospital

Right
View of the western facade looking toward the convent's main entry and chapel

Right
An early architect's sketch of the chapel interior

Opposite
Clerestory windows opposite bring the northern light in, opening the room to the heavens

Right
An architect's model of the convent, showing the two internal cloisters and the northern glass face of the chapel

Left
The plan is simple, organised around
two central cloisters and incorporating
the existing residence into the scheme

Below
The stained-glass windows of the chapel,
inherited from the previous convent, and
towering clerestory remain unnoticeable
until evening when light from the religious
services within casts a heavenly glow

Right
Set well back from the busy residential street, the building is restrained and fits in with the natural setting. Simple and minimal materials mark the exterior

Below
Suggestive of the protective hand of God, the angular wall provides a sense of safety to the sisters who sit and worship in the rows of pews beneath

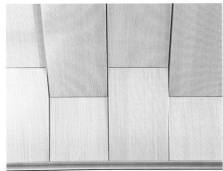

Above
Tucked behind the chapel, the ante-room glistens with opalescent glass tiles affixed to the ceiling and the century-old stained-glass window which bathes the room in warm light

Convent for the Sisterhood of St John the Divine

learn
Study

Places of education are, by function, incubators of new ideas and testing grounds where accepted truisms and conventions are frequently challenged. While this is largely a by-product of exploration, inquiry and debate, the potential of architecture as a means for learning about both ourselves and the city in which we live must not be discounted. Toronto is a city largely known for simple modernist lines driven by a slight fear of the avant-garde. The academic projects in this chapter, however, challenge our collective consciousness, forcing us to question not only the role of architecture but to redefine the typical Toronto style.

learn *Study*

A popular adage reads, 'When the student is ready, the master will appear'. An appropriate design corollary might well be, 'When the city is ready, the building will appear'. As an urban microcosm of a city that is indeed ready, the St George campus at the University of Toronto has unarguably raised the bar by assembling a showcase of contemporary urban architecture. Starting in 2001 with Graduate House, the University intentionally discarded architectural conservatism and enlisted deconstructivist architect Thom Mayne of Morphosis. As Mayne's nervously cantilevered cornice liberated itself from the constraints of its urban site and intruded into the public space of the street, the building challenged our comfort limits in the definition of public space. Although nowhere near the spectacle of Graduate House, sitting in its shadow is the Early Learning Centre, a three-storey stack of children's building blocks of brushed metal, wood, and green-tinted glass. At the other end of the spectrum, the Bahen Centre for Information Technology by local architects Diamond + Schmitt relies on its good manners to become a confident yet somewhat humble neighbour. A mature example of urban infill, the Bahen is a perfectly-scaled complement to an already lively campus ensemble.

While the ubiquitous 'glass box' of the 1960s and '70s often takes the blame for stealing a city's soul, two modernist events – for to simply call them buildings belies their impact – prove that this is not always the case. Toronto-based architectsAlliance in joint venture with Germany's Behnisch Architekten used their Terrence Donnelly Centre for Cellular and Biomolecular Research to reconnect an abandoned campus pathway. The 12-storey glass cube revels in its slick aesthetic, while at the same time it is one of the most 'green' buildings in the city. Immediately beside it, Foster and Partners' Leslie L Dan Pharmacy Building is an equally sophisticated glass cube, which also features two mammoth silvery pods suspended precariously inside the atrium. As the fritted glass box sits aglow in its urban forecourt, the ovoid pods offer themselves as signposts to both the University and the 'Discovery District', one of the most concentrated clusters of research and medical institutions worldwide.

A number of independent learning-based projects beyond the University of Toronto's gates have also sold the virtues of clean lines and simple forms to an enlightened and ready population. As the city's modest temple on the hill, the Canadian National Institute for the Blind is modern in its lines but also intentionally unassuming; preferring

instead to quietly blend in. But this is precisely the point as, like its
residents, it simply wants to be like everybody else. At York University,
on former farmlands north of Toronto, the Schulich School of Business
taps into the region's agrarian sensibility with rounded corners and a
subtle material palette of cut limestone and vertical panels of
opalescent-hued clear and frosted glass.

Equally influential are the collective works of Toronto architects
Kuwabara Payne McKenna Blumberg. The firm has risen to become
one of Toronto's most prolific architectural studios and has played a
large part in shaping the city's recent architectural growth spurt. Their
Royal Conservatory of Music sits virtually at the epicentre of the city's
renaissance and provides much needed performance and academic
space for Canada's premier music and arts educator. In the same
modern style, the new home for Canada's National Ballet School is a
perfect injection of culture and attitude to an area suffering from urban
neglect.

No doubt the face of greater Toronto is changing rapidly, but so
too is the way we view our city. Our collective temperament has
matured greatly in just a few short years. Well over the initial shock of
Graduate House and armed with a new-found and progressive
appreciation for design, we are beginning to understand the lesson of
Will Alsop's Sharp Centre for Design at the Ontario College of Art and
Design. Affectionately known as the Tabletop, we accept that a
pixellated slab hovering high above the street on pencil-thin coloured
stilts is not simply a self-indulgent pursuit for spectacle, but instead
welcome Alsop's challenge to be aware of the city around us rather
than remain indifferent to its spaces. If, in the end, this is all that
education – and architecture – ever sought from us as students, then
we have certainly made the grade.

Bahen Centre for Informatio

Diamond + Schmitt Architects Inc

St George Street Campus, Toronto   2002

project

Bahen Centre for Information Technology, University of Toronto

40 St George Street, Toronto, Ontario

architect

Diamond + Schmitt Architects Inc

telephone

+1 416 978 8634

website

www.utoronto.ca

opening hours

not available

neighbourhood

tightly wedged between seven existing buildings on the sprawling University of Toronto's St George campus

style

a modest smooth-textured, ivory clay brick exterior housing an equally minimal interior of dark wood screens, stucco walls, frosted green glass and polished concrete columns

clientele

home to two of the University's primary faculties, Applied Science and Engineering, and Arts and Sciences

signature experience

standing beneath the cylindrical, illuminated metal and glass stair as it ascends a full eight storeys through the building's core

other projects

The Jewish Community Centre, New York; Israeli Foreign Ministry, Jerusalem

While sustainable design is generally accepted as the right thing to do, its value is often considered only in terms of quantitative returns such as energy performance or payback period. However, a more holistic approach suggests that sustainability must encompass many threads, both building and civic, working together to realise a qualitative common good and not just individual measurable segments. In this light, a building's sustainability should therefore be understood both for its technological solutions as well as its ability to positively contribute to the city as a whole.

The Bahen Centre for Information Technology (BCIT) at the University of Toronto is just such a building. Tightly wedged between seven existing buildings, two of which are listed as heritage properties, and having three distinct city-street facades, the BCIT is a complex urban infill project that contributes to the longevity of the campus by creating vital pedestrian connections and by offering a series of open landscaped plazas and courts on what was once neglected, marginalised land. That the BCIT takes seriously its role in helping to create a sustainable urban fabric comes as no surprise, as architect Jack Diamond first made a name for himself in the 1970s by advocating an adaptive modernism and promoting the development of mixed-use human-scaled residential projects in the heart of the city. And while credit must be given to the commitment of the architects, the facility was largely made possible by the Government of Ontario's SuperBuild programme and significant donations from John and Margaret Bahen and eBay co-founder Jeffrey Skoll.

At approximately 45,000 square metres (53,820 square yards), the BCIT is one of the largest faculties on the downtown campus, yet it is still a relatively unassuming building. This is partly due to the fact that it shares its site with two heritage buildings: the Beaux-Arts style Koffler Student Services Centre (originally the city's main reference library, designed by Chapman & Oxley in 1909) and a dilapidated yet culturally significant Victorian home. Rather than pursuing demolition or imposing itself on the block with an overbearing architectural style, the designers responded with an effective – and typically Torontonian – move by creating appropriate setbacks and mimicking the heights to create a confident but somewhat humble neighbour. The brick edifice wraps itself around the house at mid-block, then breaks free of its own mass in the form of a five-storey pavilion. Confidently defining the street corner, and then animating it with glass platforms cantilevered over the street, dissolving glazed corners, and free-floating brick panels that slip past each other, the pavilion is a perfectly-scaled complement to an already lively campus ensemble.

Right

Bahen is a complex urban infill project that contributes to the longevity of the campus by creating vital pedestrian connections and a series of open landscaped plazas on a once neglected site

Bahen Centre for Information Technology

Left
Computer rendering of the St George facade. Rather than imposing itself on the block, the warm tan brick and glass of the pavilion nicely suits the scale and feel of the street

Left
Even though it is one of the largest faculties on the downtown campus, the architects mimicked the adjacent building heights and used a variety of forms and facade details to create a confident yet humble infill project

learn
Study

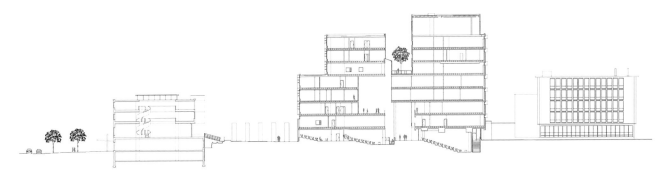

Above
Bahen stitches together a complex set
of passive and active green features
including a green roof and vegetated
terraces within the internal atrium

Below
The central concourse is a three-storey
sky-lit atrium that bisects the block and
rises to capture the once exterior brick
wall of the adjacent Koffler Centre. At
the atrium's epicentre, a cylindrical metal
and glass staircase thrusts itself upward
for a full eight storeys

In an equally modest gesture, the skin is a smooth-textured, ivory clay brick with sand-coloured, precast-concrete details that complement the heritage feel of the block. To avoid being overly monochromatic, splashes of colour from deep blue tinted glazing and a grid of sandblasted aluminium sunshades provide a subtle yet refined layer to the composition.

The BCIT was commissioned to meet the growing needs of two of the University's primary faculties, Applied Science and Engineering, and Arts and Sciences. With the hope that its multidisciplinary teaching spaces would lead to a cross-pollination of ideas, the building features 11 shared lecture theatres, 50 laboratories, an auditorium, and various specialist research facilities for computer and electrical science alongside electrical, mechanical and industrial engineering. Inside, the spontaneous interactions between colleagues are facilitated mainly in the central concourse, a three-storey sky-lit atrium that bisects the block and rises to capture the once exterior restored brick wall of the adjacent Koffler Centre. At the atrium's epicentre, a cylindrical metal and glass staircase thrusts itself upward for a full eight storeys. Encircling a frosted glass tower of stacked meeting rooms, the effect is pure drama as the stair's underpanels and the textured glass spire are set aglow by bright white fibreoptic lighting. Beyond the high-tech light show, the material palette is intentionally minimal with dark wood screens, stucco walls, frosted green glass and polished concrete columns. Overhead, the exposed concrete deck has been detailed with an undulating wave pattern offering a hint of whimsical texture.

As the BCIT snakes its way through the site, it also stitches together a complex set of passive and active green features. At the southern entrance, a new outdoor court is shaded with mature trees and cooled with active water elements, both fed by retained stormwater, while a green roof and vegetated terrace on level seven provides added energy savings via insulation and shading. Internally, careful planning guarantees that no room which requires natural light is more than 25 metres (82 feet) away from a natural source, while computer labs which require reduced glare are clustered along the minimally glazed north facade. The building is also designed to realise a high degree of internal flexibility for the future as all power, communication and ventilation services are delivered through accessible floor slabs.

As much as the BCIT illustrates that a building can be both functional but also provide for the greater good of the city, it is also a reminder that we must embrace our duty of stewardship. Beyond the obvious benefits to the environment and to future generations, the project has allowed the University to double its enrolment in its high demand IT programmes and has served as a recruiting tool attracting the very best faculty from Canada and around the world.

Opposite
When viewed from College Street, the Bahen is understood both for its technological solutions as well as its ability to positively contribute to the city as a whole

Below
Bahen confidently relates to the street by animating it with glass platforms cantilevered over the street, dissolving glazed corners, and free-floating brick panels that slip past each other

Above
Textural and layered, Bahen offers up an interesting mix of contextually sensitive clay brick and modern glass curtain wall

Right
The building's skin is a smooth-textured ivory brick with sand-coloured precast concrete details that acknowledge the heritage feel of the block, its perfectly scaled corner pavilion complementing an already lively campus ensemble

learn **Study**

Below
At 45,000 square metres (53,820 square
yards), the Bahen Centre is one of the
largest faculties on the downtown campus, yet it is still a relatively unassuming
addition to St George Avenue

learn Study

Above
Skylights and clerestory lightwells
ensure that no room requiring daylight
is more than 25 metres (82 feet) away
from a natural source

Right
The building snakes its way through
the site, tightly wedged between seven
existing buildings on the sprawling
University of Toronto St George campus

Canada's National Ballet School

Kuwabara Payne McKenna Blumberg Architects / Goldsmith Borgal and Company Architects

North Jarvis, Toronto   2006

project

Canada's National Ballet School

400 Jarvis Street, Toronto, Ontario

architect

Kuwabara Payne McKenna Blumberg Architects in joint venture with Goldsmith Borgal and Company Architects

telephone

+1 416 964 3780

website

www.nbs-enb.ca

opening hours

not available

neighbourhood

in the historic downtown North Jarvis community

style

intriguing blend of solid historical buildings and transparent contemporary pavilions

clientele

150 talented ballet students from across Canada

signature experience

watching students perform exercises at the *barres* for the audience passing by on Jarvis Street below

other projects

Le Quartier Concordia, Montreal; Canadian Embassy, Berlin

During the late nineteenth century, Toronto was home to a burgeoning industrial economy that brought with it great wealth and a wonderful medley of Gothic Revival mansions and Victorian city homes. Unfortunately, the once proud Jarvis Street in the city's east side has suffered from urban neglect and its stately residences have often fallen by way of the wrecker's ball. In an area prime for renewal, Canada's National Ballet School's (NBS) new home is the perfect injection of culture and attitude.

Based on the masterplan by Philip Goldsmith of Goldsmith Borgal & Company Architects, the design concept was to seamlessly integrate old and new players as an ensemble piece of dance training, academic and residence facilities. Sharing the site are a new and separately developed twin-tower condominium project, and two heritage structures taken over by the NBS including the original 1898 home of Havergal Ladies' College and Northfield House, once home to Sir Oliver Mowat, Ontario's longest serving Premier and a father of Confederation. Collectively, the ensemble adds a sense of legitimacy to both an art form and a neighbourhood seeking validation.

The project is the physical realisation of NBS' holistic philosophy that considers the body, the mind, and the spirit of both the dancer and of the city. At one time, these heritage buildings would have been removed to make way for modern insertions, their value seen only in the land they occupied. Today, they are respected and incorporated as a vital piece in the broader process of city building. The nexus of the project is the original 1856 Northfield House. Fully restored to its neoclassical glory, the house now contains the administrative offices. While Northfield House proudly projects its historic tale from centre stage, the new facility is located in the glass and stone Celia Franca Centre. Wrapping itself asymmetrically around three sides of Northfield House, the crisp glass wings act as a shimmering backdrop against the textured ecru brick and restored cornice moulding of the house. To the south and just off-stage is the American Queen Anne-style Havergal Ladies' College, now restored as the Margaret McCain Academic Building. Connected by a fritted-glass bridge, the new space contains classrooms, photography and science labs, an art studio, and a two-storey music room.

As is typical with Toronto's approach to modernism, the building plays the good neighbour and politely respects its context. Serving as solid bookends, the north and south facades are clad in softly coloured precast masonry, set as a random collage to soften its appearance on the street. But it is on the street face where we are reminded that all the world is indeed a stage. In the north pavilion are 12 generously scaled dance

Opposite
Passers-by are granted a rare backstage pass as images of dancers floating effortlessly by animate the space of the street

learn
Study

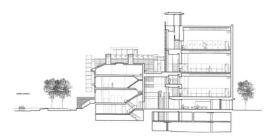

Left

Stacked vertically, three of the generously scaled dance studios provide students with dramatic outward views, setting the city as their perpetual audience

Left

The design concept was to integrate old and new players as an ensemble piece of dance training, academic and residence facilities

learn
Study

Right
As Northfield House proudly projects its historic tale from centre stage, the plan wraps itself asymmetrically around on three sides and features the Town Square, a three-storey, light-filled atrium where students socialise and interact

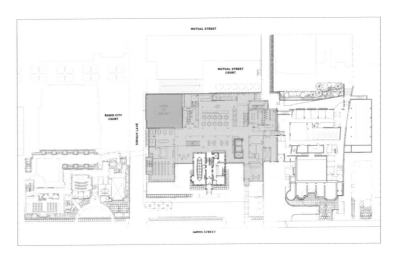

Above
The glass facade of the south pavilion is etched with a subtle frit pattern based on an excerpt of *The Nutcracker*. Written in Benesh script – a method of dance notation that traces human movement – the skin doubles as a theatrical scrim as silhouettes trace behind the backlit veil

Opposite
Wrapping itself asymmetrically around three sides, the crisp transparent new wings form a shimmering backdrop against the textured ecru brick and restored cornice moulding of Northfield House

studios. Three overlooking Jarvis Street are fitted with floor-to-ceiling glass and provide students with dramatic outward views, setting the city as their perpetual audience. But in a gesture back to the city, passers-by are also granted a rare backstage pass as images of dancers floating effortlessly by animate the space of the street. Designed by KPMB architect Mitchell Hall, the studios also feature custom wooden ballet *barres*, whose elongated ovoid form encourages the students to rest lightly while training. In the more intimately scaled south pavilion, which houses the Resource Centre, and student council offices, the glass facade is etched with a subtle frit pattern based on an excerpt from *The Nutcracker*; a Christmas tradition for generations of children. Written in Benesh script – a method of dance notation that traces human movement – the skin doubles as a theatrical scrim where silhouettes trace behind the backlit veil. It's a subtle device but very effectively tells the story of NBS and its role in promoting culture within the city.

Understanding the importance of down-time for a student's social and emotional well-being, a number of intimate, off-stage events have also been designed. In the residual space between the old and new buildings, the architects created the Town Square, a three-storey, light-filled venue where students are encouraged to socialise and interact. Appropriately, the Town Square is the nexus of the design from which all key programmes radiate including the student café, resource centre and dance studios.

While there is no doubt that ballet has a long historical lineage, the expression of the details is a very contemporary event. In the Town Square, the restored brick of Northfield House is contrasted against light oak flooring, a Corten steel fireplace and a massive projection screen for special performance events. Elsewhere, crisp white chairs and off-white tables share the space with splashes of colour that dance about in the form of green feature walls and multicoloured loungers. Moving vertically through the stacked rehearsal spaces is an equally theatrical event. The open-riser stairs emphasise the theme of lightness and have a movement and cadence of their own, while the wooden treads are soft underfoot. On the second level, a modern sculpted stair with crimson red flooring connects the studios with the student lounge. Side and under panels of frosted glass are lit from within and, like the dancers, the stairs seem to float through the space.

The Jarvis Street Campus represents the first phase of NBS' grand vision, titled Project Grand Jeté. Phase II will see the restoration and conversion of their existing Maitland Street facilities into student residences. When complete, the entire ensemble of new and restored buildings will be evidence of what ballet insiders already know – that NBS is on a par with the world's best.

Above
The frosted glass side and under panels
of the sculpted staircase are lit from
within and, like the dancers, seem to
float through the space

Left
In the residual space between the
old and new buildings, the architects
created the Town Square – a three-
storey, light-filled venue where students
are encouraged to socialise and interact

Above
In the north pavilion are 12 generously scaled dance studios. Three are fitted with floor-to-ceiling glass providing students with dramatic outward views of the city and a wonderful naturally lit environment in which to practice

Right
Sharing the site are a new, separately developed twin-tower condominium and two heritage structures, including the original 1898 home of Havergal Ladies' College, and Northfield House, the 1856 mansion built for Sir Oliver Mowat

Right
The studios feature custom wooden
ballet *barres*, whose elongated ovoid
form encourages the students to rest
lightly while training

Left
Although decidedly modern in its clean lines and horizontal banding, the CNIB intentionally makes no bold statement about its new home

Above
The architects welcomed the challenge to create a universally accessible building of, and for, all the senses for the enjoyment of people of all abilities

Right
Architect's rendering of the main entry. The city's modest temple on the hill is typified by clean horizontal lines and contemporary materials

learn
Study

Sweeny Sterling Finlayson & Co / Shore Tilbe Irwin & Partners

Bayview Avenue, Toronto   2004

The education of architects teaches students to comprehend the physical environment from many different perspectives, to continually adapt to changing conditions, to explore the tactile qualities of materials, and to interpret light and shadow to inform a vision about how we experience our environment. In so many ways, this lifelong process of visualisation, seeing beyond what our eyes tell us, parallels the daily reality of the visually impaired. So when charged with the task of designing the CNIB's new training and teaching facility, the architects welcomed the challenge to create a universally accessible building of, and for, all the senses for the enjoyment of people of all abilities.

Founded in 1918 as a voluntary agency, the CNIB is Canada's primary provider of support services, assisting people who are visually impaired or deafblind to lead independent lives. Evolving from an institution that simply provided shelter and make-work projects to one now dedicated to training and education that strives to integrate people back into the workforce, the CNIB has been a permanent fixture on the site since the early 1950s. The land was originally the home of Sunnybrook Farms owned by Joseph Kilgour, a well-to-do Toronto businessman with a love for thoroughbreds. Including a verdant deciduous and pine ravine on what was once 'Millionaires Alley', the plinth-like site is still a prominent feature in the city fabric.

It was this heroic stance overlooking Bayview Avenue that helped inform the exterior architecture of the new building. The original building was an unassuming 1950s brick fortress; a calamitous maze of corridors and dim light that offered few incentives for restoration. So, in keeping with the desire of the CNIB to be viewed as a progressive and state-of-the-art organisation, the old building was demolished and replaced with a decisively modernist response, typified by clean horizontal lines and a classic palette of charcoal brick and ochre limestone, galvanised metal and clear bands of horizontal glass. The facade also incorporates a translucent skin designed to reduce glare on the workspaces inside; a critical aspect given that 90 per cent of the CNIB users have some visual capacity.

But don't be fooled by what you see. Beyond the simplicity of the exterior, inside is a highly considered design that has less to do with visual aesthetics than it does with fully understanding the relationship of a body in space. By incorporating colour, texture, aromas and acoustics in every aspect from the smallest electrical outlet to the sound of shoes on a textured floor, or to the echoes that waft through the corridors, this is entirely about fostering freedom and independence.

Planned for clarity and familiarity, a perfectly straight central corridor repeats itself on every floor and is wide enough to allow three people or two people with a guide dog to pass freely. At the lifts, stair landings, and wall edges, the highly polished cream-coloured stone switches to a dark

project
Canadian National Institute for the Blind
1929 Bayview Avenue, Toronto, Ontario

architect
Sweeny Sterling Finlayson & Co in joint venture with Shore Tilbe Irwin & Partners

telephone
+1 416 486 2500

website
www.cnib.ca

opening hours
not available

neighbourhood
overlooking Bayview Avenue, at the former site of Sunnybrook Farms

style
the city's modest temple on the hill, typified by clean horizontal lines of ochre limestone, galvanised metal and bands of clear glass

clientele
the visually impaired and deafblind individuals of all abilities

signature experience
standing outdoors, using all your senses to guide you in the direction of the northern Shade Garden, the landscaped entry court, or the Fragrant Garden

other projects
Sweeny Sterling Finlayson & Co:
Seven Oaks Apartments, Toronto
Shore Tilbe Irwin & Partners:
Toronto Police Services Building, #52 Division, Toronto; Chemical Sciences Building, Trent University, Peterborough, Ontario

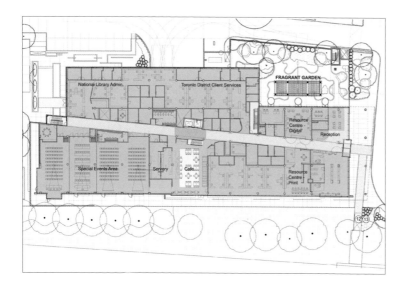

Left
Planned for clarity and familiarity, the dead-straight corridor is wide enough to allow three people or two people with a guide dog to pass freely

and more patterned field. The colour and texture of the walls also changes from white to warm cherry-wood at key navigation points, as do the door frames and baseboards to aid in wayfinding and recognition of building elements. Beyond raised text, Braille signage and tactile building maps, users can also obtain an electronic card that activates audio messages telling them exactly where they are. No detail is left unconsidered as nosings on stair treads change colour, handrails are ergonomically correct, audible devices warn of impending hazards, and even the light switch plates are of a contrasting hue. And if you can't see it, of course you will be able to feel or hear it, as materials underfoot change from hard tile to soft carpet, while also changing their ability to reflect or absorb sound depending on the zone and use.

In the centre of the space is the great room, a double-height space which houses the cafeteria and an open steel and glass stair. Flooded with natural light from floor-to-ceiling windows, and softened via an undulating textured wood ceiling, the lounge serves as a naturally lit orientation point within the building. It also opens itself up to an outdoor terrace on the west side. The historical connection with nature is strong given the proximity to the verdant ravine. In fact, one original feature that has remained since the 1950s is the famous Fragrant Garden, relocated at the building's north end. Set within curving concrete planters, the perennial garden offers a veritable bouquet of smells, textures and, of course, sounds created as the wind passes through the leaves.

Programmatically, the new headquarters brings together the four key partners that make up the CNIB organisation; the National Office, the Ontario Division, the National Library for the Blind and the Toronto District office. With their expanded role as educator, the CNIB also plays host to Canada's most comprehensive and technologically advanced electronic library; the roots of which trace back to the grandchild of Edgar Robinson and his original bequest of Braille books in 1908. Here, every major news publication will be available digitally every day in large print, speech and Braille format along with a vast selection of talking books available both on CD and through the Internet. The library also features a demonstration area where clients can be fitted with vision aids.

While the CNIB may in fact be the physical realisation of the popular maxim 'God is in the details', it still remains a relatively modest temple on the hill. The architecture is quite unassuming; it makes no bold statement about its new home and is designed largely around common sense. But this is precisely the point. Preferring instead to be ordinary, to quietly blend in and not draw attention to itself or its users, it really just wants to be like everybody else.

Above
Taking a heroic stance overlooking Bayview Avenue, the site was originally the home of Sunnybrook Farms owned by Joseph Kilgour, a well-to-do Toronto businessman with a love for thorough-breds

Right
Set within curving concrete planters, the Fragrant Garden offers a veritable bouquet of smells, textures and sounds created as the wind passes through the leaves

Right
By incorporating colour, texture, aromas and acoustics in the smallest of details, the building fosters freedom and independence

Right
A linear central corridor repeats itself on every floor. To define the wall edges, the highly polished cream-coloured stone switches to a dark and more patterned field

Below
With architecture that is relatively unassuming, the CNIB is designed largely around common sense

Left
The modernist building is typified by a classic palette of charcoal brick and ochre limestone, galvanised metal and clear bands of horizontal glass

Opposite
Flooded with natural light from floor-to-ceiling windows, and softened via an undulating textured wood ceiling, the cafeteria serves as a naturally lit orientation point within the building

Teeple Architects Inc

St George Campus, Toronto   2003

project
Early Learning Centre, University of Toronto
7 Glen Morris Street, Toronto, Ontario

architect
Teeple Architects Inc

telephone
+1 416 978 6725

website
www.utoronto.ca

opening hours
Mon – Fri: 8 am to 6 pm

neighbourhood
nestled on a quiet, leafy street in the heart of the University of Toronto's St George campus

style
a cubic structure of corrugateded aluminium panels and glass resembling a stack of children's building blocks

clientele
an exploration space for the young children of University of Toronto students and faculty, and university students involved in research in early childhood development

signature experience
daydreaming in your own miniature child-size loft, overlooking the playroom and your classmates below

other projects
St Joseph Media Office, Toronto; Pickering West Branch Library, Pickering, Ontario

In education, constructivist theory suggests that learning is an active process in which knowledge is developed on the basis of experience. What we experience, physically and socially, and how we perceive those events ultimately forms our own personal realities. What better way then, to enhance the learning of young, inquisitive minds, than to set them free in a space that promotes interaction, experimentation and discovery? The Early Learning Centre at the University of Toronto is such a space.

Nestled on a leafy street, this three-storey research and childcare facility is an intriguing playground for its young inhabitants. Completed in 2003, the facility provides daycare for 102 children of the University of Toronto faculty, staff and students, from infants to pre-school age. Teeple Architects, a local Toronto firm with extensive experience in building childcare centres, designed the 1250-square-metre (1495 square yards) facility. The structure aims to provide both support services for university faculty and student families, and an educational and research facility for students doing work in speech pathology, physiotherapy, rehabilitation or fieldwork placement in childhood development.

From the exterior, the structure resembles a stack of children's building blocks, with a seemingly random collection of varying volumes and room heights, irregular window openings, and exterior and interior spaces. Yet the building remains innocuous, with a scale and muted material palette of brushed metal, wood, and green-tinted glass well suited to the residential setting. Occupying a modest-sized lot, the horizontal plane, moderate height and contemporary details of the building could lead it to be mistaken for a modern home rather than the progressive educational facility that it is. Extensive glazing punctuates the exterior, allowing the youngsters to connect with the world outside and offering passers-by a glimpse of the activities inside. Respectful of the site, an existing walnut tree has been incorporated into the building's design, providing ample shade for the delightful play space along the south facade.

Inside, each floor is centred on a multipurpose play area where the children can gather and interact. Grouped around this are age-specific rooms for the infants, toddlers, and pre-schoolers resident in the daycare facility. Sleeping nooks, changing rooms, stroller lockers and other spaces necessary to serve the young inhabitants are found throughout. The glass connections continue inside, providing visibility in and out of rooms, and up and down between floors.

Moving through the space, it unfolds before you as a modernist version of a jungle gym. There are places built for climbing, for exploring, for playing, and for resting. The rooms are open, light-filled spaces with hardwood floors and pastel-coloured walls, a soothing backdrop against which to dream and create. A long wide ramp, perfect for small footsteps, connects the two main floors. Venture upwards and a surprise awaits:

oronto

Right
Occupying a modest-sized lot, the horizontal planes, moderate height and contemporary details of the building could lead it to being mistaken for a modern home

Early Learning Centre

Left
The playrooms are open, light-filled spaces with hardwood floors and pastel-coloured walls, a soothing backdrop against which to dream and create

Left
On the premise that exposure to natural light improves scholastic performance, extensive glazing is found throughout the centre

learn
Study

Right
A long wide ramp, perfect for small footsteps, connects the two main floors

Above
Modest in scale, the building offers
a muted material palette of brushed
metal, wood, and green-tinted glass
well suited to the residential setting

Opposite
Numerous interior windows allow staff
and researchers to inconspicuously
make their observations and monitor
the activities of the children

quiet and active play spaces have been built outdoors on the multi-level rooftops. With glass walls and overlooking the street below, a child would be easily entranced by the magic of this private treehouse.

Architect Stephen Teeple has been purposeful in creating not just rooms in which to learn, but using the physical structure of the rooms themselves to promote learning. Sunken floor niches provide intimate spaces for the children to play together and grasp their first lessons on sharing. Miniature child-sized lofts, raised five steps above ground, are a perfect place for quiet contemplation, or a space to build an imaginary fort below. The needs of staff and researchers are similarly addressed, as the numerous interior windows allow them to inconspicuously make their observations and monitor the activities of the children. Virtually every surface in the building begs to be explored, and the variety of spatial experiences truly sets the imagination of the young users free.

The multitude of windows is used to great effect, maximising daylight and bringing the outdoors in. Studies have shown that the benefits of natural light must never be underestimated, especially in a classroom setting. Students experience more positive moods and tend to perform better scholastically in classrooms with natural light. Fittingly, all playrooms in the Centre have windows. As well, the central ramp rises in a double-height atrium, with light cascading from the skylights above. Clerestory windows highlight the roof line and allow light to permeate the building.

The Early Learning Centre sits in the shadow of Graduate House, also built by Stephen Teeple in joint venture with Thom Mayne of Morphosis. While Graduate House is more imposing in form, the two buildings certainly push the envelope of thinking on space. Experience them, and you too may learn a lesson

Below
Sitting in the shadow of Graduate House,
the building blends in nicely with the
scale of the surrounding streets, despite
its geometry and modern details

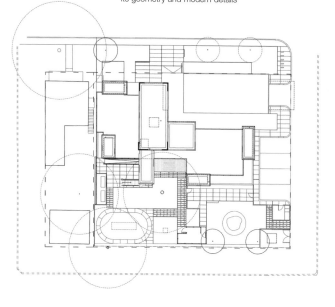

Above
An existing walnut tree has been
incorporated into the building's design,
providing ample shade for the delightful
play space along the south facade

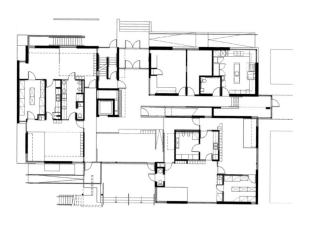

Left
Internally, each floor is centred on a
multi-purpose play area where all the
children can gather and interact, with
age-specific rooms for the resident
infants, toddlers, and pre-schoolers
grouped around it

Left
At the core of the plan, the central ramp
rises in a double-height atrium with light
cascading from the skylights above.
Clerestory windows highlight the roof line
and allow light to permeate the building

learn
Study

Above
Miniature child-sized lofts, raised five
steps above ground, are a perfect place
for quiet contemplation, or a space to
build an imaginary fort below

Left
Extensive glazing punctuates the exterior,
allowing the youngsters to connect with
the world outside and offering passers-by
a glimpse of the activities inside

Graduate House
University of Toronto

Morphosis Inc / Teeple Architects Inc

St George Campus, Toronto   2006

project

Graduate House, University of Toronto

60 Harbord Street, Toronto, Ontario

architect

Morphosis Inc in joint venture with Teeple Architects Inc

telephone

+1 416 946 8888

website

www.sgs.utoronto.ca/gradhouse

opening hours

not available

neighbourhood

at the gateway to the University of Toronto downtown campus

style

skins of charcoal-coloured concrete and perforated metal advance, wrap and then retreat to expose the solidity of the structure below

clientele

a diverse, multicultural community of 400 graduate students

signature experience

feeling nervous standing under the Big O

other projects

Morphosis: Diamond Ranch High School, Pomona, Ontario; San Francisco Federal Building, San Francisco, USA

Teeple Architects Inc: Scrivener Square, Toronto; Ajax Main Central Library, Ajax, Ontario

Progressive cities around the world long to own a signature building of recognised calibre, one that will solidify its presence on the world cultural scene. You only have to think of Bilbao to fully understand the impact of landing a coveted work by Frank Gehry or Norman Foster. Of course, Toronto has finally brought Gehry to the Art Gallery of Ontario, secured Foster in the Leslie L Dan Pharmacy Building, and attracted some of architecture's brightest stars to spearhead its renaissance; yet it was just a few short years ago that deconstructivist Thom Mayne of Morphosis delivered an iconic project, that at the time was the most avant-garde building the city had seen in decades.

Graduate House – a graduate student residence at the University of Toronto – was the first-born of a campus-wide redevelopment initiative by the university. Determined to reassert itself within the city fabric and also as a player on the international stage, the mandate was clear: the University was seeking a 'landmark' gateway project. In winning the international open-competition, Mayne, together with Toronto architect Stephen Teeple, rejuvenated an often neglected building type (the student residence) and, given the cultural climate at the time, caused consternation among professionals, and agitated local residents.

Programmatically the *parti* is quite simple – it is essentially a standard apartment block. Architecturally, however, it expresses itself as four separate urban elements that wrap a sunken courtyard, a reflecting pool and terrace, all accessible from the pavement. Accommodation for 433 students is provided in three- and four-bedroom apartments impressively arranged in combinations of single- and two-storey units. The facade, although tame by Mayne's own admission, is every bit a Morphosis event. In a fashion never before seen in Toronto, skins of charcoal-coloured concrete banding and broad sheets of perforated metal advance, wrap and then retreat to expose the solids of the structure below.

At the centre of the debate, however, is what has become known as the Big O. Unlike the traditional vocabulary of the conventional framed gateway (arches or symmetrical pillars), the transparent band is simultaneously threshold, structure and sign. The 'O' is actually the last letter in a giant illuminated marquee in which the words 'University of Toronto' are ghosted on to backlit green-fritted glass. Challenging the generally accepted terms of the building-to-street relationship, the nervously cantilevered cornice is liberated from its site to freely shoot through and intrude into the public space of the street. In a move specifically designed to challenge the prevailing conservative cultural

Right

Positioned at a critical point of transition between civic and academic space, Graduate House willingly serves as a physical and theoretical portal between living and learning; between city and campus

206

Left
Layers of charcoal-coloured concrete banding and broad sheets of perforated metal advance, wrap and then retreat to expose the solid structure beneath

Graduate House

Right
The building consists of four separate
urban elements that wrap a sunken
courtyard, a reflecting pool and terrace,
all accessible from the pavement

Below
The quartet of materials and forms are
of a scale and mass that differ appropriately according to the conditions of the
facing street

Above
Accommodation for 433 students is
provided in three- and four-bedroom
apartments impressively arranged in
combinations of single- and two-storey
units

Opposite
For the international open-competition
to build the Graduate House, the mandate was clear: the university was seeking a 'landmark' gateway project

mindset, Teeple suggests the project was 'about the fine line between the urbanistically responsible and something that … disturbs, that breaks through the responsible guideline'.

While Mayne sees the humour in the sign, the local opposition bewilders him as well. 'This is the edge … it is a symbol of the university. What more appropriate place to demonstrate the power of architecture?' He laments, 'in architectonic cities like Vienna or Paris, this would be nothing unusual, where arches, bridges, and tunnels complicate and enrich the space … [Graduate House] does what university buildings ought to do, push the envelope and experiment with ideas'. Ultimately Mayne was correct; it just took Toronto a few years to realise this because for all the civic anxiety and media attention it gathered, Graduate House now looks tame when compared with Will Alsop's Tabletop at the Ontario College of Art. It's amazing how much the city has matured, both physically and culturally, in just five short years.

Public opinion notwithstanding, the most salient quality of Graduate House is an understanding of its metropolitan presence. Moving beyond its pragmatic role as a residence, it skilfully uses its form and orientation to play a greater urban role. Positioned at a critical point of transition between city and campus, and armed with a desire to challenge public complacency, it welcomes the opportunity to serve as a physical and theoretical portal between living and learning.

Too often campus housing has been relegated to the role of background fabric. Here, Mayne and Teeple have restored the front-lines position of the residence typology and, in doing so, re-established the necessary dialogue between the university and the city. Graduate House also delivers many of the essential elements necessary for the realisation of a coherent urban ensemble. Through a sequence of events, the public space of the street is allowed to filter through a grade-level transparent café, which in turn addresses the semi-private space of the courtyard. Moreover, the quartet of forms are of a scale and mass that differ appropriately according to the conditions of the facing street.

An adage reads, 'When the pupil is ready, the master will appear'. The appropriate design corollary might well read, 'When the city is ready, the building will appear'. Rising to slay the dragon that is banal institutional architecture, Graduate House can revel as a signature piece that responds to the synergies of urban and academic life. Comprehensible as a whole, yet understood as something more than the sum of its parts, it provides an interconnected atmosphere of physical and social exchange that spans both city and campus.

Above
Known affectionately as the Big O, the
O is actually the last letter in a giant illu-
minated marquee in which the words
'University of Toronto' are ghosted onto
backlit green-fritted glass

Right
The nervously cantilevered cornice is
liberated from its site to freely shoot
through and intrude into the public
space of the street

learn
Study

Right
Programmatically the plan is quite simple,
being essentially a standard apartment
block. Accommodation for over 400
students is provided in three- and four-
bedroom apartments cleverly arranged in
combinations of single- and two-storey
units

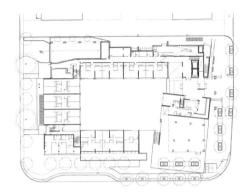

Graduate House

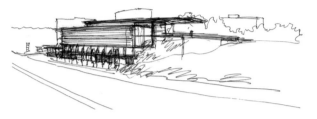

Left
Architect's early sketch illustrating the strong horizontal lines set against the gently sloping site

Above
The building accentuates the high-speed course of the street with two horizontal blocks imbued with a motion of their own through a high-performance skin of shiny metal and glass

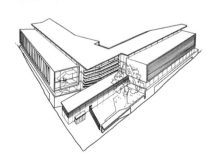

Right
Laid out in a broad 'V' formation, the main volumes are set above a retaining wall. At the corner, as the street falls off into the ravine, the blocks frame an outdoor plaza

learn
Study

nd Technology Centre
Centennial College

Kuwabara Payne McKenna Blumberg Architects

Morningside Avenue, Toronto   2004

For all the remarkable architecture that is changing the face of downtown Toronto, it is important to remember that in a true *Design City* not all gems need be in the urban core and that sometimes, great architecture can find a home in the marginalised outer fringes. In a somewhat banal suburban zone defined by high-speed arterials and retail strips, a local community college has taken the term 'community' literally and created a much needed focal and gathering point for the north-east Toronto suburb.

The Centennial HP Science and Technology Centre is Centennial College's newest home for their health science programmes, as well as engineering technology and media. The project was driven in part by a government mandate to strengthen the relationship between community colleges and universities. Not that the college needed to work on its academic connections as it already has a long-standing history as an educational provider within the city. The centre is, however, the first new building the school has constructed in 25 years and is now home to over 3500 full-time students who collectively speak more than 80 languages. If Toronto is truly a mosaic of cultures, then the college is indeed a microcosm of this condition and certainly more than just a post-secondary training facility. Conceived under the creative eye of KPMB team-leaders Bruce Kuwabara, Shirley Blumberg and Paulo Rocha, in association with designers at Stone McQuire Vogt Architects, the project creates a self-sufficient academic village. The 22,000-square-metre (26,300 square yards) facility includes classrooms, a cafeteria, over 50 computer and specialised laboratories, a generously proportioned naturally-lit interior, and landscaped exterior spaces where students and faculty members can linger, socialise and interact.

Situated at the intersection of Morningside and Ellesmere Avenues within the Scarborough Campus of the University of Toronto, the building's success at making connections comes in the way it relates to the space of the street. Nestled tightly against the rising contours of the nearby Highland Creek tablelands, and with little urban context to respond to, the building accentuates the high-speed nature of the street with two horizontal blocks imbued with a motion of their own. Through a high performance skin of shiny metal and glass, the building is laid out in a broad 'V' formation, the wings of which are set atop a retaining wall plinth of dark charcoal-coloured brick. At the corner, with the two horizontal bars hovering in space as the street falls off into the ravine, the narrow edges of polished aluminium and glass frame the borders of an outdoor plaza and frame a transparent gateway into the central atrium beyond. In its final urban act, the entire glazed corner shifts and kinks and then bursts outward and upward as if to make a bold and defiant gesture against the banalities of suburbia and its lack of recognisable iconic architecture.

Moving inside, the beating heart of the centre is the dramatic internal Town Square. A nexus for all student activity including the resource centre

project
Centennial HP Science and Technology Centre, Centennial College
755 Morningside Avenue, Toronto, Ontario

architect
Kuwabara Payne McKenna Blumberg Architects

telephone
+1 416 289 5300

website
www.centennialcollege.ca

opening hours
not available

neighbourhood
Scarborough, a north Toronto suburb with a diverse immigrant population

style
shooting forms of charcoal brick, polished aluminium and a shiny skin of metal and glass

clientele
health sciences, business and engineering students

signature experience
sitting on the pseudo-Spanish Steps beneath the suspended wooden lecture theatre

other projects
Jackson-Triggs Winery, Niagara-on-the-Lake, Ontario; Design Exchange, Toronto

and café, the Town Square is a four-storey open atrium, fully glazed on the
southwest to capture the bright summer light but also the warm autumn
colours from the adjacent ravine. Inside, the designers have intentionally
tapped into one of Europe's most successful urban moments for social
gathering: the Spanish Steps in Rome. Taking full advantage of the
changing topography, the raked concrete steps rise a full two storeys, and
provide a fanciful hang-out for students or additionally for formal
assemblies and graduation ceremonies.

Undoubtedly though, the signature experience must be standing
beneath the massive wood volume that hovers above a sea of stark white
café tables and chairs. Precariously perched on kinked concrete columns,
the box – affectionately dubbed the Egg – contains the main lecture halls
and classrooms. Clad in Douglas fir with knife-cut detailing, the golden
wood skin warms what is an otherwise utilitarian palette of steel structure,
poured concrete columns and floors, and white walls accented with
swatches of blue ceramic tiles. While the block does slice itself open on
the south face to expose student lounges within, on the north face the
thick wood skin frames a stark face of metal frit where back-lit silhouettes
of students randomly appear against the gloss-white interior walls.

An excellent example of the Toronto style of modernism in that it
marries raw industrial materials with serious awareness of its site and the
needs of its users, the building is not without its humour. Granted it
responds to our love affair with speed through its elongated facades, it
then makes a playful jab at suburban car-culture as those who take the
bus are rewarded with the fantastic experience of coming in directly under
the Egg, while those who drive are forced to enter through a more
subdued back door.

This is a very responsible design move that makes an equally strong
statement about edge-city architecture. With suburbia often criticised for
its unsustainable qualities, the building achieves some very notable green
gains. The exposed concrete floors use their thermal mass to capture and
retain heat energy while being durable and low-maintenance. Additionally,
the vast expanses of south-facing glass capture natural light, yet are
shaded by computer-controlled horizontal and vertical louvres and fritted
glass panels. To accommodate the transient nature of students and the
ever-changing programmatic requirements, the building's generic rooms
can easily be transformed to accommodate a variety of different curricula.
And in a very fitting move, Centennial College has proactively launched in
this facility a full-time architectural technology programme specialising in
sustainable building design and construction.

Right
The horizontal blocks forming the main
core of the building are set on both
sides on retaining wall plinths of dark
charcoal-coloured brick

Centennial HP Science and Technology Centre

Left
The centre is the first new building that Centennial College has constructed in 25 years and is now home to over 3500 full-time students who collectively speak over 80 languages

Left
The 22,000 square metre academic centre includes over 50 computer and specialty labs

Below
Precariously perched on kinked concrete columns with knife-cut styling, the hovering wooden volume contains the main lecture halls and classrooms

Above
The building's generic rooms can easily be transformed to accommodate a variety of different curricula

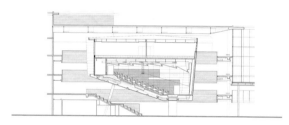

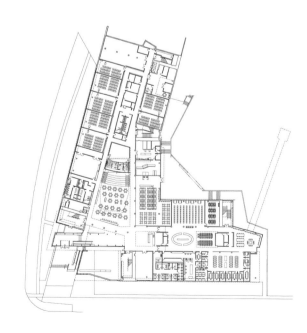

Right
The college is laid out to function as a self-sufficient academic village. The central square at the kink of the 'V' is the nexus for all student activity including the resource centre and café

learn**Study**

Right
The golden wood skin of the Egg
warms what is an otherwise utilitarian
palette of steel structure, poured concrete columns and floors, and white
walls

Left
Generously proportioned and naturally
lit interior spaces allow students and
faculty to linger, socialise and interact

Centennial HP Science and Technology Centre

Above
Like the Spanish Steps in Rome, the raked concrete steps rise a full two-storeys, and provide a fanciful hang-out for students

Right
The dramatic Town Square is the nexus for all student activity including the resource centre and café and features a four-storey open atrium, fully glazed on the southwest to capture the light and weather of the changing seasons

Right
Vast expanses of south-facing glass
capture natural light, yet are shaded
by computer-controlled horizontal and
vertical louvres and fritted glass panels

Leslie L Dan Pharmacy Building

Foster and Partners / Moffat Kinoshita Architects / NXL Architects

College Street, Toronto   2006

project

Leslie L Dan Pharmacy Building, University of Toronto

144 College Street, Toronto, Ontario

architect

Foster and Partners in joint venture with Moffat Kinoshita Architects and NXL Architects

telephone

+1 416 978 2889

website

www.pharmacy.utoronto.ca

opening hours

not available

neighbourhood

In the university's Discovery District, alongside the Medical and Related Sciences Centre, and Terrence Donnelly CCBR

style

a sophisticated glass box injected with a touch of technological whimsy

clientele

240 students in the university's under graduate pharmacy programme

signature experience

standing atop the ovoid pod hovering within the 16-storey atrium

other projects

Foster and Partners:

Swiss Re Headquarters, London : Hearst Headquarters, New York

Moffat Kinoshta Architects:

School of Communications Management, Ryerson University, Toronto

If higher learning teaches us anything, it is that we must never accept events at face value and always strive to look deeper. At first glance, it would be easy to believe that the newest addition to the University of Toronto, at the corner of Queen's Park Circle and College Street, is yet another typical example of modernist architecture – the ubiquitous 'glass box'. But think again, for this is no ordinary building and its designer is certainly not your average architect.

The Leslie L Dan Pharmacy Building is the brainchild of Norman Foster, England's most renowned designer. While Foster and his 600-person 'studio' is responsible for some of the most prominent buildings in London since 2000 including the Great Court of the British Museum, Millennium Bridge, Greater London Assembly Building and the Swiss Re Building (ubiquitously known as 'the Gherkin'), this represents his first Toronto commission, although, since winning the competition, he has subsequently taken on projects in Calgary and Vancouver. Foster is also a recipient of the Pritzker Prize, architecture's most prestigious award bestowed upon a living architect for a distinguished portfolio of completed work. The award brings enormous international prestige and represents a who's who of architecture including Frank Gehry who is currently leaving his signature on the Art Gallery of Ontario, and Thom Mayne of University of Toronto's Graduate House fame.

It is no surprise that the University of Toronto attracted Foster to the project. In the span of less than five years, the list of star architects who have landed at the campus has virtually exploded, including Germany's Stefan Behnisch who designed the highly sophisticated Terrence Donnelly Centre for Cellular and Biomolecular Research on a site immediately adjacent. The fact that the commission for a simple faculty building was put out as an international design competition meant the university was serious. Additionally, that 23 international firms including Foster even responded to the call was a clear signal that the buzz about the city's architectural renaissance was reaching international ears. Partnering with local practices Moffat Kinoshita Architects (which has since been purchased by Cannon Design) and NXL Architects, the CA$70 million project was funded jointly by the Ontario Government's SuperBuild fund and through a lead gift by Leslie L Dan, a known scientist, entrepreneur and philanthropist, as well as an alumnus of the University.

Home to over 1000 undergraduate and postgraduate students, thus creating the largest pharmacy faculty in Canada, the building itself is intended to be seen not only as a gateway to the University but also to the Discovery District, one of the most concentrated clusters of research and medical institutions worldwide. What makes this building so interesting is that Foster shows us that iconic works do not necessarily have to be blatantly garish. Set well back from the corner, the 12-storey building literally floats 20 metres (65 feet) above its forecourt on worryingly slender

Left
The Pharmacy Building is a handsome
addition to the city's urban fabric and
sits nicely within its urban forecourt

Below
Standing directly underneath the free-
floating orbs is indeed a heart-stopping
experience

Leslie L Dan Pharmacy Building

Left
Set well back from the corner, the building literally floats 20 metres (65 feet) above its forecourt on a grid of slender concrete columns called *pilotis*

Right
The top of one of the orbs is sliced away providing an open lounge space for students and faculty, and also an absolutely spectacular view of the city beyond

Above
The glass facade is somewhat subdued and typically modernist with its blue glass panels and its unique white dot-frit pattern embedded within the glass

Opposite
The real drama is saved for the two mammoth silvery pods suspended precariously in mid-air. The ovoid orbs contain lecture and reading rooms

concrete columns, or *pilotis*, and a five-storey wall of Belgian glass that allows uninterrupted views in and out to the adjacent heritage buildings. Basically a box on top of a box, it is actually a very respectful solution, as the height of the lower cube mimics the height of the surrounding buildings and the nearby Ontario Parliament. When viewed from the corner, the neighbouring Centre for Cellular and Biomolecular Research disappears behind, while their two plazas merge to grant Foster's glowing lantern a truly iconic position within the newly created larger urban square.

From the outside, the facade is somewhat subdued and typically modernist with its blue glass panels and grid of metal mullions. Yet a unique white dot-frit pattern embedded within the glass adds a layer of dimension when backlight at night as the facade dissolves away, exposing the open labs at the north-east corner. And while it's not immediately obvious, Foster still manages to land a hearty one-two punch on the inside. Towering a full 16 storeys (14 storeys above and two storeys below ground), a colossal slot slices through the core of the building. This towering daylit space is the nexus of activity allowing fluid movement between floors, to the library and wet labs above, but also the lecture theatres two levels below. As expected, the materials are slick and utilitarian; grey stone floors, open riser stairs with wood and glass rails, and silver-coated accent panels are found throughout.

But the real delight is saved for the two mammoth silvery pods suspended precariously in mid-air. The ovoid orbs contain lecture and reading rooms; the larger of the two holding 60 students with the smaller being a classroom for 25. The top of one of the orbs is sliced away providing an open lounge space for students and faculty, and also an absolutely spectacular view of the city beyond. If standing directly underneath the free-floating orb is not a heart-stopping experience, then crossing a narrow catwalk to have a coffee atop the second while hovering within the 16-storey atrium must surely be.

For most local architects it was inconceivable that the city would, within half a decade, play host to Frank Gehry, Daniel Libeskind, Will Alsop and the UK's most celebrated architect, Sir Norman Foster. The unthinkable has indeed happened and they are coming in droves. And while the Pharmacy Building may not have the iconic wow-factor of Libeskind's Crystal at the Royal Ontario Museum, or the drama of Alsop's Tabletop at the Ontario College of Art and Design, it is a handsome addition to the city's urban fabric, and hopefully not the last we will see of Foster.

Above
Towering a full 16 storeys, a colossal
slot slices through the core of the
building. Inside, two mammoth silvery
pods, suspended precariously in mid-
air, contain lecture and reading rooms

Right
The central atrium is the nexus of activity
allowing fluid movement between floors,
to the library and wet labs above, but
also to the lecture theatres two levels
below

Below
As expected, the materials in the atrium
are slick and utilitarian; grey stone floors,
open riser stairs with wood and glass
rails, and silver-coated accent panels
throughout

Right
Glowing deep red within the main lobby, the ovoid orbs contain lecture and reading rooms; the larger of the two holding 60 students, and the smaller being a classroom for 25

Below
It would be easy to believe that the newest addition to the University of Toronto, at the corner of Queen's Park Crescent and College Street, is another typical glass box. But this is no ordinary building and its designer is certainly not your average architect

Leslie L Dan Pharmacy Building

Sharp Centre for Design
Ontario Colleg

Robbie/Young + Wright Architects / Alsop Architects
McCaul Avenue, Toronto   2003

project

Sharp Centre for Design, Ontario College of Art & Design
100 McCaul Street, Toronto, Ontario

architect
Robbie/Young + Wright Architects in joint venture with Alsop Architects

telephone
+1 416 977 6000

website
www.ocad.ca

opening hours
Mon – Fri: 7.30am to 12.00 midnight
Sat: 8.45am to 6.00pm
Sun: 12.00 midday to 12:00 midnight

neighbourhood
in a leafy downtown neighbourhood, near the Art Gallery of Ontario and surrounding galleries

style
a whimsical pixelated slab perched high above the street on massive slender stilts

clientele
artists, filmmakers, and designers-in-training

signature experience
standing underneath the tabletop at dusk as ultraviolet night-lights cast an ephemeral glow

other projects
Alsop Architects: Peckham Library, London: North Greenwich Jubilee Line Station, London
Robbie/Young + Wright Architects: Rogers Centre (Skydome), Toronto ; Rexall Centre, York University, Toronto

Most artists and architects would agree that when it comes to a critic's opinion about their work, there is nothing worse than indifference. This is particularly true in architecture, as a building is meant not only to define and provide functional space, but also to generate emotions, feelings and sentiment within the hearts and souls of those who use its spaces on a daily basis. So perhaps then, the success of a building should not be measured against budget, schedule or how well it incorporates program, but rather how strong an emotional response it creates, whether it is positive or negative.

Like it or not, most everyone will agree that the Sharp Centre for Design at the Ontario College of Art & Design (OCAD) will never be the victim of indifference. Yet this is exactly where the gritty urban school of both fine and applied arts wants to be, residing somewhere in the indeterminate zone between respectful politeness and in-your-face, exuberant rebellion against uniformity and sameness.

Located just north of the trendy shopping blocks of Queen Street West, the Sharp Centre is undoubtedly the most avant-garde building this city has seen since Viljo Revel landed with his curvaceous city hall in 1965. Affectionately known as the Tabletop, the building is just that; a massive two-storey slab perched some 27 metres (88 feet) above the street on 12 slender stilts that look more like colourful crayons. In actuality, the main support for the building comes from the jet-black monolithic elevator core rising from the heart of the original brick building, with most of the crayons being more of a whimsical reference to the arts. Wrapping the entire slab equally on all sides is a metal skin painted with a black and white dot matrix pattern interspersed with a seemingly random pattern of punched openings. By day, the white hulk looms overhead, while at night, ultraviolet lighting gives the slab an ephemeral presence from afar.

While all this drama may seem like a solo statement about a shameless pursuit for urban spectacle, architect Will Alsop vehemently denounces its iconic status, and contends that there is a much deeper message conveyed here. The Tabletop is really the physical realisation of the broader mandate for the school in that it teaches us to be aware rather than indifferent to the world around us. But if the building's exterior exemplifies 'what' the school is about, the interior is equally aware of the 'who' – the art students. The Tabletop is actually one small part of the OCAD's campus redevelopment and expansion initiative, which included a significant amount of interior renovation to effectively tie the old and new together in a series of classrooms and studios. In the residual space between the two original brick buildings off McCaul Avenue, sits the entry foyer, a four-storey atrium naturally lit through alternating bands of clear, coloured and frosted glass. One level up, the space opens into the Great Hall, a two-storey volume that doubles as gallery and student gathering space. Here, the mass of the black core doubles as a projection surface

f Art & Design

Right
Early conceptual sketches of the scheme illustrate Alsop's talent as an architect, an art educator and a painter.

Above
Wrapping the entire slab equally on all sides is a metal skin painted with a black and white dot matrix pattern interspersed with a seemingly random pattern of punched openings

for students in the film media program. A giant 'X' of fluorescent pink neon, and a number of playful coloured blobs also in fluorescent pink, actually glow in the dark and are inset into the crisp, all-white ceiling. Crossing the space, a set of bridges clad in angular, knife-cut patterned panels connect the two original school buildings and are lit from a series of chrome theatrical light gantries suspended overhead.

Left

A new plaza underneath the Tabletop will form a natural link with Grange Park and the Art Gallery of Ontario on one side and downtown Toronto on the other

learn **Study**

Right
The height of the building was intentionally set so that most of the condominium
residents across the street would not
lose their views of the park beyond

Above
The main support for the building
comes from the jet-black elevator core
rising from the original brick building,
with most of the crayons being more
of a whimsical reference to the arts

Opposite
The Sharp Centre for Design stands
near another Toronto icon, the CN
Tower, the world's tallest free-standing
structure

On the two upper floors, which house the classrooms and north-
facing studios, the interiors are far more austere and make little reference
to the dramatic exterior, save for deeply set tinted windows with coloured
surrounds that double as seating alcoves for daydreaming, and another
albeit smaller pink 'X' incised in the ceiling. Perhaps the best part of the
studios though is that vast sections of the oversized steel framing are left
exposed and free to be man-handled, a treat for those who watched the
massive substructure being erected during the summer months.

Interestingly, in a city known for its preference for polite and refined
modernism, the Sharp Centre with all of its shock value and spectacle has
surprisingly found a following of ardent admirers. It could be that the
building is completely exhilarating to be under and is just slightly insane;
or it could be that it is simply fun to imagine that one day it might just up
and walk away. It is likely though, that people have come to understand
that this seemingly irrational design is actually a very sensitive and
thoughtful urban scheme. On the site where a parking lot once sprawled,
and where yet another average glass box might have risen, there is now
a fully landscaped urban 'parkette' that connects with Grange Park, the
historic greenspace tied into the Art Gallery of Ontario, currently getting its
own makeover by Frank Gehry. Equally, the height of the building was
intentionally set so that most of the condominium residents across the
street would not lose their views of the park beyond.

While this may be his first North American commission, Alsop is
hardly a new kid on the block, having honed his skills for decades as an
architect, an art educator and a prolific painter for many years in Britain. In
fact, during the early stages of the design, Alsop held design charettes
with the local community and asked that they paint their perception of
what the building should look like. Alsop's joint venture partner, Robbie/
Young + Wright are no strangers to success either, having designed
SkyDome (renamed the Rogers Centre), the first sports and entertainment
stadium with a retractable roof.

While Alsop himself admits that it is his best work to date, he is
reluctant to classify the Sharp Centre as a progeny of any particular style,
although 'slabs on legs' is a predominant theme in his portfolio. Regardless
of the influence, many have credited The Tabletop as being the springboard
for Toronto's architectural renaissance, a movement which, thanks in part
to the Provincial Government's SuperBuild endowment fund, is radically
transforming the city's urban and cultural landscape, and with it, reshaping
our definition of the quintessential Toronto style.

Above
Known as The Tabletop, the building is a massive two-storey slab perched 27 metres (88 feet) above the street on 12 slender stilts that look more like colourful crayons

Right
By day, the white hulk looms overhead, while at night ultraviolet lighting gives the slab an ephemeral presence from afar

Right
Residing somewhere between respectful
politeness and in-your-face, exuberant
rebellion, The Tabletop is the physical
realisation of the school's mandate to
avoid indifference of the world around us

Right
Seen from the east, the whimsical black and white pixelated slab is punctuated by glowing window cut-outs and floats high above the street on massive slender stilts

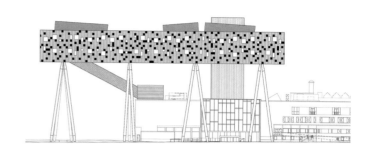

Right
A section through the building shows the relationship of the tabletop to the existing buildings below. On the two upper floors are the classrooms and north-facing studios

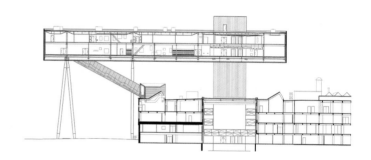

Below
The entry foyer consists of a four-storey atrium naturally lit through alternating bands of clear, coloured and frosted glass

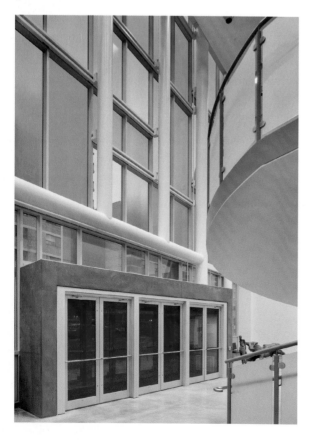

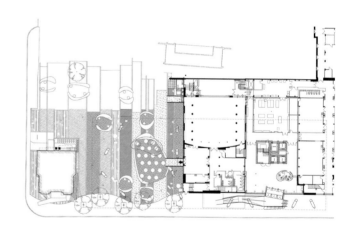

Above
On the site where a parking lot once sprawled, there is now a fully landscaped urban plaza that connects with Grange Park, the historic greenspace tied into the Art Gallery of Ontario

Opposite
A giant 'X' of fluorescent pink neon and a number of playful coloured blobs are inset into the all-white ceiling of the Great Hall

learn
Study

Below
The project is a subtle amalgamation of both historic preservation and modern insertion and intentionally acts as a layered backdrop to the historic High Victorian McMaster Hall and adjacent Romanesque Mazzoleni Hall

Right
Set against the Royal Ontario Museum, the conservatory seems tame, although it is a mature and modern addition to the Bloor Streetscape

learn
Study

or Performance and Learning

Kuwabara Payne McKenna Blumberg Architects

Bloor Street, Toronto   2007

Founded in 1886 as an independent school dedicated to music and vocal training, the humble roots of the original Toronto Conservatory of Music can be traced back to the second floor of a small music store at Yonge Street and Dundas Street. The first of its kind in Canada, the Royal Conservatory of Music (RCM), as it is now known, has grown exponentially over the years to become Canada's premier music and arts educator.

From its prominent home within the Bloor Street cultural precinct, the TELUS Centre for Performance and Learning is perfectly positioned both physically and educationally at the epicentre of the city's renaissance. Currently under construction at the time of this writing, the expansion and renovation project will provide much needed performance and academic space, but more importantly will pronounce the RCM's status as a global innovator in the musical arts. Of course, the fact that it is located immediately adjacent to the Royal Ontario Museum, currently undergoing its own renaissance at the hands of star architect Daniel Libeskind, will only increase its international appeal. The ROM notwithstanding, the school is actually located on an important piece of urban real estate within the city, being just a stone's throw away from the historic University of Toronto campus and several other cultural institutions including Moriyama and Teshima's origami-esque Bata Shoe Museum and the newly renovated Gardiner Museum of Ceramic Art, also by KPMB.

With over 70 design awards, KPMB is one of Toronto's most lauded architectural studios and has played a large part in shaping the city's recent architectural growth spurt. Led by partner Marianne McKenna, and associate Bob Sims, the project is a subtle amalgamation of both historic preservation and modern insertion. Featuring a new 1000-seat concert hall, performance studios, rehearsal hall, and library, the architecture actually makes its strongest urban statement by being quietly polite. Although the new predominantly glazed pavilions are significant in size and scale, they make no attempt to compete for presence on Bloor Street but, instead, intentionally act as layered backdrops preserving the integrity of the historic High Victorian McMaster Hall (1881) and adjacent Romanesque Mazzoleni Hall (1901).

While the rich red brick facades will be restored to their former glory, the most salient gesture to the street is a soft-spoken, wood and glass pavilion. Acting as the western counterpoint to the existing Mazzoleni Hall to the east, the pavilion completes the overall urban composition by framing McMaster Hall and helping to define the new landscaped forecourt. Serving as one of several formal points of entry, the modest wooden edifice also houses a rehearsal room for the orchestra and allows for off-stage social moments for students. This belies its greater role as this spot is actually the launching point for a more fluid procession that carries visitors along a public promenade that meanders through the site,

project
TELUS Centre for Performance and Learning, Royal Conservatory of Music
273 Bloor Street Street, Toronto, Ontario

architect
Kuwabara Payne McKenna Blumberg Architects

telephone
+1 416 408 2824

website
www.rcmusic.ca

opening hours
to be completed 2007

neighbourhood
alongside the museums and boutiques of stylish Bloor Street

style
a duet of Victorian grandeur and refined modernism

clientele
gifted young singers, musicians, faculty, and supporters of the arts

signature experience
listening to the soft sounds of music reverberate along the glass bridges linking the old and new wings

other projects
Centre for Genomics and Proteomics, McGill University, Montreal, Quebec; Art Gallery of Hamilton, Hamilton, Ontario

Left
In the rehearsal hall, a contemporary
palette of rich wood, stainless steel and
glass will contrast with the deep red
brick of the existing heritage buildings

Below
The building wraps itself around a set
of existing historic buildings and also
establishes strong urban relationships
with both Bloor Street to the north and
Philosopher's Walk to the east

Above
Sitting on a red brick podium and fully
glazed on three facades, the multistorey illuminated concert hall will provide spectacular views of Philosopher's
Walk and the city skyline beyond

past a small café and then on to the new concert hall. Within the multi-storey, skylit promenade, a network of contemporary steel and glass bridges and catwalks traverse the space to link the old and new wings. Along the way, the integration of old and new becomes immediately apparent as a contemporary palette of rich wood, stainless steel and glass, unfolds and overlaps around the historic brick and stone detailing. At the opposite end, the concourse opens itself up and connects to the adjacent Philosopher's Walk, a verdant pathway that winds itself southward from Bloor Street.

The completion of the journey is the reception lobby and concert hall. Sitting on a red brick podium and fully glazed on three sides, the multistorey illuminated jewel-box will provide spectacular views of Philosopher's Walk and the city skyline beyond. More importantly, it will also hold its own as a modern counterforce to the exaggerated styling of the Royal Ontario Museum.

The heart of the project, without a doubt though, will be the new Michael and Sonja Koerner Concert Hall. Conceived by the architects as the physical realisation of the RCM's mission to nurture the vital role of music in our society, the hall will be on a par with similar performance spaces in New York and London. Nestled snugly between the glazed concourse to the north and practice/lounge spaces on its ends, the modern hall blends in comfortably within the heritage context of the site. Modelled in the classical 'shoe-box' style, the hall is a tall rectangular room with high ceilings and three storeys of continuous wooden-faced balcony seating. Overhead, an undulating veil of wooden ribbons adds texture and contributes to the overall acoustics.

To date, the RCM has realised over 70 per cent of its initial financial campaign. This is significant in that it undeniably validates the city's collective commitment and new-found public appreciation for music and design and underscores the value in their marriage, especially if a metropolis aims to call itself a true *Design City*.

Right
Within the multistorey skylit cafeteria, a network of contemporary steel and glass bridges and catwalks traverse the space to link the old and new wings

Below
East-west section through the main performance hall

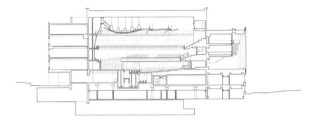

Left
Modelled in the classical 'shoe-box' style, the heart of the project will be the new Michael and Sonja Koerner Concert Hall. Overhead, an undulating veil of wooden ribbons will add texture and contribute to the overall acoustics

Below
The facility is a gentle Modernist addition to the sprawling campus, located on former farmlands north of Toronto

learn
Study

School of Business
York University

Hariri Pontarini Architects / Robbie/Young + Wright Architects

Keele Street, Toronto   2004

The Schulich School of Business is ranked as the best business school in Canada by *Forbes*, the *Financial Times* of London, and *The Economist*. It is ranked 13th in the world by *The Wall Street Journal* and third among non-US schools by *Forbes*.[1] With a reputation for innovative programming and a global focus, Schulich attracts a diverse international student population. How fitting then that such a programme is housed in a facility which is also recognised as world-class.

Awarded with the prestigious 2006 Governor General's Medal in Architecture, the complex at York University's Keele Street campus is made up of the Seymour Schulich Building and the adjoining Executive Learning Centre. The Governor General's Medals are Canada's highest honour, given in recognition of outstanding achievement in projects by Canadian architects. Built by Hariri Pontarini Architects, in joint venture with Robbie/Young + Wright Architects, the building is the culmination of a highly collaborative process between designers, students, staff, and faculty.

With the awarding of SuperBuild funding from the Ontario government in 2000, the project team set out on a challenging process that would take them to research over 100 different business schools. Best practices were identified – from the latest developments in wireless technology, classroom layout, and instructional technologies, to the impacts of natural sunlight and office design. To ensure that the end product would ultimately meet the needs of the user community, a series of full-day workshops were held with the Schulich students and staff throughout the programming and design phases. For a business school which fosters group work and team development at every turn, the Schulich School is a brilliant example of how collective thinking often leads to superior results.

On the exterior, Schulich's rounded corners, soft lines, and subtle palette are a welcome contrast to York's harder-edged buildings like Vari Hall, with its soaring brick rotunda, and the low-slung Central Square, marked by the giant orange steel I-beam sculpture at its entry. Horizontal bands of cut limestone are juxtaposed against random vertical panels of clear and opalescent-hued frosted glass. Heavy copper mullions add order and structure to the impressive curtain wall. At three storeys and 31,500 square metres (37,675 square yards), the facility is a gentle modernist addition to the sprawling campus located on former farmlands north of Toronto. The adjacent wood lot and three landscaped courtyards surround the building with a sense of calm and refuge from the bustle of campus life.

The undulating, agrarian feel of the exterior meets with crisp lines and hard textures on the interior. Materials are simple and muted, with an abundance of stone, wood, concrete, white walls, and frosted glass dominating the space. Despite the hard edges, the school is both flexible and fluid in utility. Field research identified that the world's best business

project
   Schulich School of Business, York University
   4700 Keele Street, Toronto, Ontario

architect
   Hariri Pontarini Architects in joint venture with Robbie/Young + Wright Architects

telephone
   +1 416 736 2100

website
   www.schulich.yorku.ca

opening hours
   not available

neighbourhood
   on the sprawling suburban York University campus

style
   a continuous, undulating ribbon of cut limestone, glass, and heavy-gauge copper details

clientele
   top Canadian and international business students, faculty and visiting executives

signature experience
   enjoying casual conversation with Canada's business elite in the central Marketplace

other projects
   Hariri Pontarini Architects: McKinsey & Company, Toronto; MacLaren Art Centre, Barrie, Ontario
   Robbie/Young + Wright Architects: Wickaninnish Inn, Tofino, British Columbia

Opposite
Horizontal bands of cut limestone are
juxtaposed against random vertical
panels of opalescent-hued frosted glass
while heavy copper mullions add order
and structure

schools shared two common characteristics: first, a way to bring people
together and promote interaction; and second, more private and personal
spaces for contemplation and study. The Schulich School achieves both
admirably, with a building that meets the needs of not only today's but also
tomorrow's business leaders.

At the hub of the structure is the vast and airy CIBC Marketplace.
This soaring three-storey atrium features a café where students can catch
the latest business reports broadcast on the giant projection screen. The
building's main entry and exit points and corridors to the classrooms and
faculty offices all flow seamlessly into this central space, leading to a
cross-pollination of ideas across the multi-generational students and staff.
Moving away from the nexus, the spaces become quieter but no more
solitary. Unassigned spaces abound, marked by floating chairs, benches,
and built-in ledges, ready to accommodate impromptu meetings.
Classrooms of all types, from small team meeting rooms to large lecture
halls, line the passageways. Faculty offices are accessible and are
organised in neighbourhood clusters, each with their own reception areas
and service spaces. As requested by the user groups, most of the spaces
feature glass walls and windows that open, allowing an abundance of
natural daylight and fresh breezes to stimulate young minds.

With a diverse population that includes young undergraduates,
visiting executives, and mature MBA students balancing studies and
work, the Schulich School needed to convey the best in business
environments. Like the downtown skyscrapers in which some of these
students hope to some day work, the building has all the technological
niceties including interactive IT teaching labs, a computer drop-in site, and

Below
The adjacent wood lot and three landscaped courtyards provide a sense of
calm and refuge from the bustle of
campus life

Left
The School's rounded corners, soft lines
and subtle material palette stand in contrast to York's harder-edged buildings

learn
Study

a high-tech library research centre, ensuring that these future business leaders have access to the online world at every turn. Visiting lecturers and corporate executives will feel just as comfortable in the 300-seat Robert R McEwen Auditorium which features translation booths, a green room, and a tiered amphitheatre outfitted in stylish tones of grey and linen.

The Executive Learning Centre (ELC) complements the main building with a more sophisticated palette for its corporate students. With a unique combination of educational environment and residential dwelling, the ELC services business executives and corporations to their exacting standards. The boutique hotel-type tower offers every amenity the globe-trotting executive expects: 60 stylish guest suites with built-in work areas, a private boardroom, office suites, a fitness facility, a penthouse lounge with panoramic views, and an ever-helpful concierge. The executive dining room, an elegant double-height space that can accommodate 275 seats for private dining or gala events, also offers the classmates room to mingle during their free time.

Whether working in teams in the many break-out rooms or sitting alone in the lecture halls, the school is a flexible responsive space. Despite occupying a building characterised by cramped and poorly organised spaces for its first 30 years, the Schulich School of Business was still able to build a reputation as a world-class institution. In this dazzling new home, you can only imagine what the next 30 years will bring.

1   According to 2005 and 2006 global rankings.

Left
Located at York University's Keele
Street campus, the Schulich School's
architecture is a blend of modern clean
lines with a slight agrarian sensibility

The soaring three-storey atrium features a café, a giant projection screen broadcasting the latest stock market quotes and business reports, and a cantilevered concrete staircase

Above
The undulating, agrarian feel of the exterior meets with crisp lines and hard textures on the interior *(above)*, where unassigned spaces abound – marked by floating chairs, benches, and built-in ledges *(top)*, ready to accommodate impromptu meetings

Below
Inside, spaces are organised around neighbourhood clusters that relate to the internal courtyard, and include classrooms of all types, from small team meeting rooms to large lecture halls.

Opposite
The two-storey executive dining room is an elegant and modern space which can accommodate 275 seats for private dining, corporate or gala events

Terrence Donnelly Centre for Cellula

Behnisch Architekten / architectsAlliance

St George Campus, Toronto   2006

project

Terrence Donnelly Centre for Cellular and Biomolecular Research, University of Toronto

160 College Street, Toronto, Ontario

architect

Behnisch Architekten in joint venture with architectsAlliance

telephone

+1 416 978 8861

website

http://tdccbr.med.utoronto.ca

opening hours

not available

neighbourhood

at the centre of the Discovery District, an area housing the University of Toronto's research and medical facilities

style

an elegant 12-storey glass cube embellished with fanciful colourful glass panels

clientele

cutting-edge researchers from the Faculties of Medicine, Pharmacy and Applied Science, and Engineering

signature experience

standing in delight as you realise the coloured glass panels which dot the east facade mimic the familiar pattern of the DNA barcode

other projects

Behnisch Architekten: Genzyme Center, Cambridge, Massachusetts
architects Alliance: York University Computer Science Building, Toronto

It is very likely that few people outside the medical profession will know that Toronto is home to one of the most concentrated clusters of research and medical institutions worldwide. With specialities in bio-informatics and genomics, Toronto's 'Discovery District' and the adjacent Victorian-esque University of Toronto boast the fourth-largest medical research community in North America, while the University's Faculty of Medicine has been Canada's largest academic institution for 11 years running.

Attracting the best and brightest has always been a mandate for the University, so it's not surprising that an international competition to design a new research facility would attract the most innovative architectural designers as well. Awarded to Germany's Behnisch Architekten in joint venture with Toronto-based architectsAlliance, the technically-advanced Terrence Donnelly Centre for Cellular and Biomolecular Research (CCBR) is being touted as much for its 'wow factor' as it is for its ushering in a new era of scientific and architectural discovery. The fact that it sits a stone's throw from the Leslie L Dan Pharmacy Building by Foster and Partners certainly adds to the cachet of the block.

Known for an equally sophisticated and urbane approach to high-density projects, architectsAlliance has been consistently developing a strong presence in the Toronto fabric. Although neither practice had a depth of laboratory experience, their mutual appreciation for sustainable design and a collaborative design philosophy won them the commission in 2001, with construction completed four years later. The CA$105 million project was funded jointly by the Ontario government, the Canada Foundation for Innovation, the university's Infrastructure Investment Fund and through private donor support.

Behnisch firmly believes in the notion that innovative building science will be the catalyst for new architectural ideas. It is likely that the same can be said about a building's influence on architectural awareness, as the CCBR is itself a lesson in Toronto modernism. Like so many of the city's other modern icons, the 12-storey glass cube revels in its slick aesthetic and technological innovation, while politely tipping its hat to its mature counterparts. Set well back from the street, the slender elegant tower sits comfortably next to the stone bastions of higher learning that surround it on three sides, and stands proud within the newly created urban forecourt. Perched on a sloping granite berm, the full level grade change from street to front door is traversed by gentle ramps and landscaped terraces. At the seventh floor, the glass facade cuts away to create a deep reveal; in typical Toronto fashion it is a respectful homage to the existing height datum of the historic St George campus.

Decorated with a network of light and colourful glass panels, the skin is both folly and high-performance technology, with each elevation treated differently depending on the various programmatic and climatic requirements. At first glance, the dance of coloured bars across the east

nd Biomolecular Research

facade appears completely random, but it is not long before the familiar pattern of a DNA barcode becomes evident. Yet this whimsy belies the science at work here, as this is actually a high-performance double skin providing natural and passive ventilation for the labs within, as well as acting as a noise buffer. While this may seem high-tech by Canadian standards, Behnisch has already perfected the system in several projects, including the recently completed Genzyme Center in Cambridge, MA, already touted as one of the country's most environmentally sustainable office buildings. Factor in shallow, open-plan floorplates, an abundance of natural light and verdant double-height winter gardens with fig and

Below
Decorated with a network of light and colourful glass panels, the skin is both folly and high-performance technology with each elevation treated differently depending on the various programmatic and climatic requirements

Above
Three seminar rooms project into the corridor as amoeba-shaped pods, each covered with shimmering Italian glass mosaic tiles in shades of russet, beige and charcoal

learn
Study

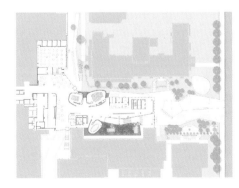

olive trees that act as oxygen-rich lungs for the building, and the CCBR becomes the teacher yet again: this time as a lesson in sustainability. In fact, the project was recently short-listed for the Lubetkin Prize by the Royal Institute of British Architects, awarded for the most outstanding building outside the EU.

What the CCBR is really about is making connections, and often between unlikely bedfellows. Residing somewhere between the historic campus structures and leading-edge technological needs, the building bridges the gaps in the form of textured wooden ramps or crisp glass and steel stairs. Moving inward, the white granite and terrazzo forecourt unfolds itself from the street edge to become a towering multistorey atrium, replete with liriope grass and bamboo. Tying into the campus's existing circulation routes, this invigorating microclimate actually encourages students to use the building as a shortcut to the nearby subway station. Again, playing the good neighbour, the architects restored the Romanesque brick facade of the adjacent Rosebrugh Building and incorporated it within the atrium. Along this meandering promenade, three seminar rooms project through as amoeba-shaped pods, each covered with shimmering Italian glass mosaic tiles in shades of russet, beige and charcoal.

But it is on the building's upper levels where the CCBR literally shines. Designed to promote the cross-fertilisation of ideas, the top 10 floors are essentially open lofts; a concept also embraced in Will Alsop's recent Queen Mary College Medical Building in the UK. With a transparent facade that affords spectacular panoramic views both in and out, and few fixed walls to define space, the labs have become a very public spectacle; a far cry from the image of scientists working behind closed doors in hermetically sealed rooms. And knowing that most breakthroughs occur outside the lab, the architects also included a number of off-stage spaces as each floor boasts a café and a communal lounge with hot-wired benches ready for every spontaneous epiphany.

Opposite
The architects restored the Romanesque
brick facade of the adjacent Rosebrugh
Building and incorporated it within the
atrium

Left
Double-height verdant winter gardens
with fig and olive trees act as oxygen-
rich lungs for the building

Above
The white granite and terrazzo forecourt
unfolds itself from the street edge to
become a towering multistorey atrium,
replete with liriope grass and bamboo

Below
The upper levels of research labs are
essentially open lofts, designed to promote the cross-fertilisation of ideas, a
concept also embraced in Will Alsop's
recent Queen Mary College Medical
Building in the United Kingdom

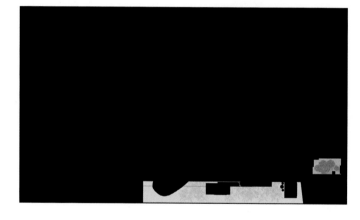

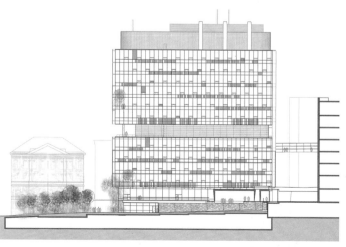

Right
Like so many of the city's other contemporary buildings, the 12-storey glass
facade is laid out in a rational grid and
is a lesson in the modernist aesthetic

learn **Study**

Below
At night, the familiar pattern of the DNA barcode is unmistakable as coloured bars become visible across the east facade

learn
Study

Right
The many double-height winter gardens
help with the natural ventilation of the
building

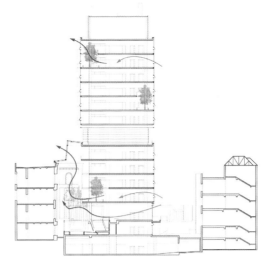

Above
The CCBR is one of the city's most
green buildings with a bamboo atrium
and double-height winter gardens

Terrence Donnelly Centre for Cellular and Biomolecular Research

253

'Torontonians display a level of openness unlikely in any city, let alone a city of Toronto's size and magnitude. It is metropolitan, yet it feels as intimate as a village. Its welcoming spirit has attracted millions of people from all corners of the world, making up a deep and culturally rich human mosaic. Toronto doesn't have a Chinatown, it has three of them ... Toronto isn't just diverse, it's the most diverse city in the world. Toronto is a culture of cultures; Torontonians celebrate humanity.' [1]

Toronto by Neighbourhood

Sitting on the shores of Lake Ontario, Toronto is a city of cultural enclaves, of architectural pockets and a wonderful mosaic of distinctive workaday neighbourhoods that stretch out in all directions from the downtown core. The glue that binds the entire city together as one modern metropolis, these neighbourhoods are truly a reflection of the diverse culture of the city and, in fact, are representative of almost every ethnic group from around the world. From rows of stone Victorian buildings in Cabbagetown to the brownfield industrial redevelopment of the Gooderham & Worts Distillery District, inside the stylish shops on Bloor-Yorkville to the funky boutiques of Queen Street West, along the waterfront condos on the Harbourfront, to the leafy homes in the Beaches, through Little Italy, Chinatown and the Gay Village – the city is alive with layers of culture, beauty and architecture.

Toronto's fabric also enjoys a virtually continuous blanket of green urban forests. So ubiquitous is this field of green, that when viewed from the city's highest vantage point at the top of the CN Tower, the city seems to disappear under the great canopy of mature growth. Formed by receding glaciers nearly 10,000 years ago, many of the natural ravines have survived to this day. Urban forests like the Don Valley and High Park feature dense, tree-lined pathways, cool running streams, 150-year-old trees, and biking trails. Respites from the bustle of city life, these vast swaths are the green fingers that stitch the city's array of residential neighbourhoods together.

Prior to 1998, the City of Toronto proper was originally part of the Metropolitan Toronto region, an area bordered by a number of outlying municipalities and towns. With amalgamation that same year, a number of these municipalities including York, East York, North York, Etobicoke, and Scarborough were brought under one political seat to become what is now known as the Greater Toronto Area (GTA). Today the GTA is one of North America's fastest-growing urban areas, consisting of four regions and 25 municipalities covering an area of over 7100 square kilometres (2740 square miles). While its geographical boundaries have grown exponentially with amalgamation, the city nevertheless remains known to many as simply Toronto.

Urban planner and theorist Jane Jacobs said it best when she suggested that Toronto's densely woven collage of urbanism and compact neighbourhoods has made it the envy of many North American cities as they chart the path to their own urban future.[2] In this chapter, we examine some of these neighbourhoods. Of an enviable human scale, most are long-standing city fixtures that have greatly influenced the shape, culture and narrative of the city while others have become recently fashionable due to gentrification and redevelopment. Tracing a path from east to west, this survey is by no means exhaustive as Toronto has over 240 distinct neighbourhoods and over 30 'Special Districts', some man-made and some inherited from nature.

Above
Much of the urban fabric is characterised by leafy streets and rows of two-
storey Victorian-era homes

The Beach

At the end of Queen Street East, about 10 minutes east of the city core,
is The Beach, an upper-middle class residential neighbourhood and a
popular summer destination for tourists. Replete with trendy shops that
line Queen Street, The Beach is famous mostly for its large waterside
parks and continuous wooden boardwalk. The beach itself is a lengthy
single stretch of sandy shoreline, but its singular name is somewhat
misleading as there are four distinct named areas: Balmy Beach,
Scarborough Beach, Kew Beach and Woodbine Beach. Although recently
there has been some debate over the official name – Beach or Beaches[3]
– most Torontonians will recognise either when describing this particular
neighbourhood. Architecturally, the neighbourhood is like many in the city,
a collage of single and semi-detached homes, low-rise apartments and
many large mansions, predominantly on the north side of Queen Street.
One structure of particular significance is the RC Harris Filtration Plant (not
featured in this volume), a robust Art Deco structure that is one of the city's
most admired buildings, yet also one of the least known to outsiders.

Cabbagetown

Like many of Toronto's residential neighbourhoods, Cabbagetown is rich
in history, culture and architecture. Located in the east end of the city,
overlooking the Don River Valley, the neighbourhood takes its name from
its original Irish immigrants who, upon moving to the area in the late
1840s, planted cabbages on the front lawns. Once a slum plagued by
poor living conditions and overwhelmed by the odorous effluvia from the
marshes of the Don River, today the area comprises the largest single area
of preserved Victorian housing in North America.[4] This was largely due to
a massive building boom in the late 1800s which saw rows of workers'
cottages, slightly more affluent semi-detached Victorian and Queen Anne,
and well-to-do Gothic Revival detached homes all built side by side.
Unfortunately, the post-war years saw much of the original housing stock

razed to make way for government assisted housing projects such as Regent Park. Today, however, Cabbagetown has experienced its own gentrification as most of its original buildings have been renovated and are now home to more affluent families. Its proximity just north of the Church and Wellesley neighbourhood, the city's vibrant gay village, has also helped foster the community pride in the area. While many of its original heritage buildings have been lost, many still remain, and because of this Cabbagetown has rightfully become the symbol for renewed urban living in Toronto.

Church and Wellesley

Toronto may have an undeserved reputation for cold winters, but it is certainly warm to the alternative lifestyles of the gay community. Located in the city's east end, near the leafy streets of historic Cabbagetown, Church and Wellesley is the city's most prominent lesbian, gay, bisexual, transsexual (LBGT) oriented community. While a number of popular monikers are used, most simply refer to the area as Church Street, since the majority of gay-related businesses are located on this stretch. Just near Wellesley, on Church, you can take a class at The 519, a newly renovated community centre by local architects Kohn Shnier, and then people-watch from the patio at Il Fornello Restaurant, as featured in the eat*Enjoy* section of this book. The neighbourhood also plays host to the country's largest annual Pride Week celebration, drawing over 800,000 people in the last weekend in June.

The Distillery District

In 1831, British Norfolk-born James Worts and brother-in-law William Gooderham set up a flourmill at the mouth of Toronto's Don River. When Gooderham realised that spirits were as much a staple as was food and shelter to the burgeoning community, he added a still in 1837. By Confederation, the distillery was producing over two million barrels of rye whisky a year and in as few as 10 years it was the largest distillery in the British Empire. Gradually, the buildings fell silent, with only one bottling line turning out amber rum until it too stopped production in 1990.

Today, to pass through the gates of revitalised Gooderham and Worts Distillery is to be transported back in time to a Dickensian world of cobblestone streets and grimy Victorian brick buildings replete with the

Right
Approached from a distance along Tankhouse Lane, the character of the Young Centre for Performing Arts is unquestionably 'industrial-chic'

Right
On what was then the water's edge, the
St Lawrence market area is replete with
a wonderful array of distinctive four-
storey Georgian, Renaissance Revival
and Victorian warehouses

still odorous relics of a long forgotten era. While Victorian factories are quite common in Europe, a site of this size and condition is a true anomaly in Canada. Located at King and Parliament Streets, a short 15-minute walk from the eastern edge of the downtown core, the area was once the epicentre of Toronto's vibrant industrial past. Of the 100 buildings that made up the original distillery, only 45 remain. Although they might be described as architecturally robust, a consistent style and an industrial elegance are revealed in the brick friezes, stone corbelling and wooden fenestration.

With obvious parallels to New York's SoHo or Vancouver's Granville Island, there has been some concern that development and gentrification will create yet another upmarket shopping district. The fact that in 1988 the 13-acre site was designated a National Historic Site should certainly help the cause. Additionally, the developers have secured a long-term lease with Artscape, a non-profit organisation dedicated to providing permanent, affordable studio space for artists and performers. Along with Artscape, the Distillery District also plays host to a variety of retail tenants including the Boiler House Restaurant and the Young Centre for Performing Arts, both featured in this book.

St Lawrence Market and Front Street East

The city began along this stretch of Front Street East when John Graves Simcoe arrived in 1793 to map out a colonial capital for Britain's new province of Upper Canada. Later rechristened York, this 10-block rectangle, on what was then the water's edge, is today replete with a wonderful array of distinctive four-storey Georgian, Renaissance Revival and Victorian warehouses. Some of the early structures were destroyed in the Great Fire of 1849, or have suffered from neglect, but many still stand, including Toronto's only remaining building with a cast iron facade. Today, most have found new life as retail stores, restaurants and loft condominiums. At the epicentre of all this history is the St Lawrence Market building, the site of the city's original market and one of two major farmers' markets in the city, the other being Kensington Market near Chinatown. Designed by Henry Bowyer Lane in 1844, the red brick behemoth has a long-standing role in the city's history as it once played home to Toronto's first permanent city hall and jail house (1845–99) and was also formerly Police Station #1. The market staved off demolition in the early 1970s and is today a Saturday morning Mecca for fresh fare and indeed an icon in the city. The market area is also home to two projects featured in this book: Izakaya can be found just west of the market on Front Street, while the Jamie Kennedy Restaurant and Wine Bar is literally just south and around the corner.

Above
The St Lawrence Market in the city's east end is a Saturday morning Mecca for fresh fare and very much a fixture in the city

The Financial District and Downtown

Like any large city, Toronto's urban core and Financial District is marked by glistening towers of concrete, glass, and steel. Centred at the intersection of King and Bay, steps away from the headquarters of Canada's five largest banks, the area offers much in the way of architecture. Four high-profile landmarks – Toronto City Hall, Commerce Court, the Eaton Centre, and the Toronto-Dominion (TD) Centre – each built in the mid-1960s, have become synonymous with the image of Toronto as a modern metropolis and still hold court as defining icons within its core. At the core is the Toronto-Dominion Centre by Mies van der Rohe. A collection of jet-black towers clad in bronze-tinted glass, the TD Centre is the city's most familiar landmark next, of course, to the CN Tower. Following the lead of the Toronto Dominion Bank, a number of other financial institutions created their own iconic spires including First Canadian Place, Canada's tallest skyscraper at 72 floors; Commerce Court for the Canadian Imperial Bank of Commerce, designed by I M Pei; the rust-coloured Scotia Plaza and the luminous gold Royal Bank Plaza. In 1992, Spanish architect Santiago Calatrava created for BCE Place a soaring six-storey galleria of interlocking white steel ribs and glass. Inside the atrium is the reconstructed 1845 facade of the Commercial Bank of Midland, Toronto's oldest surviving stone building.

Connecting many of the buildings in the financial district is a unique underground pathway. Stretching over 27 kilometres (16 miles) and featuring over 1200 retail shops and services, the PATH is the world's largest underground shopping complex according to the Guinness Book of World Records. Approximately 50 office buildings, two major department stores, six hotels, the subway transit system, and some of the city's major attractions including the Hockey Hall of Fame, Air Canada Centre and CN Tower are connected to the PATH.

Harbourfront and Queen's Quay

The stretch of Queen's Quay, between Bathurst and Jarvis Streets, marks the centre of Toronto's Harbourfront area. Historically used as the base for the city's shipping and industrial activities, the majority of today's Harbourfront was created in the late nineteenth century through lakefilling. Over the years, the area has also played home to military operations. It continues to be the recreational home for many yacht and rowing clubs which dot the shoreline, as well as the launch point for the Toronto Island ferries. Today, some remnants of Harbourfront's built heritage still remain, although many have been transformed for reuse. The Canada Malting Silos, built in 1928 by the Canada Malting Company to store malt hops, continue to stand tall at the foot of Bathurst Street, while the former Tip Top Tailors Building, one of Toronto's most significant Art Deco structures, has been converted into a loft development.

Large-scale urban planning began in earnest in the late 1970s, but the face of Harbourfront will undergo its most dramatic change in the next few years as the city places an increased focus on the renewal of the area. With the selection of the winning Toronto Waterfront Redevelopment design in May 2006, the area will hopefully explode with an intriguing mix of contemporary landscape design, recreational amenities, pedestrian areas, cultural facilities and residential buildings.

Toronto Islands

Attracting over 1.25 million visitors a year, the Toronto Islands are unarguably one of the city's best used – and vehemently defended – public parks. A small archipelago of eight tree-lined islands with over 800 acres of verdant interconnected parkland, beachfront, and residential cottages, the islands have rightfully been attracting visitors since 1833. Beyond offering today an amusement park, yacht clubs, demonstration farms, and an urban airport, the islands provide what is, without question, the best view of the city skyline, particularly at dusk when the city's skyscrapers turn a golden glow in the setting sun. The islands though weren't always so. Originally a sand spit at the mouth of the Don River, a violent storm in the late nineteenth century eradicated the land bridge at the Eastern Gap and effectively created the islands as we now know them.

Architecturally, the islands retain much of their original and unique charm. As early as 1837, hotels were established, and by 1867 a burgeoning community of tents and ramshackle wood-frame cottages functioned as a summer getaway. When the city assumed responsibility in the late 1950s, most of the cottages were expropriated and the land converted to public parks. Today, only the easternmost islands remain occupied. Vehemently defended as a vital and distinct community within the city, the islands remain home to some 450 full-time residents. Still set on a charming network of narrow, pedestrian-only streets, the collage of historic cottages and newly inserted contemporary houses is a wonderful opportunity to see an aspect of the city as it once was.

Yorkville and Bloor Street

Yorkville and the adjacent artery of Bloor Street is one of the country's most affluent urban commercial and residential districts. Roughly defined by Bloor Street to the south, Davenport Road to the north, Avenue Road to the west and Church Street to the east, Yorkville is outfitted largely with upmarket retail outlets including Prada, Gucci, Chanel and Louis Vuitton, and has become synonymous with ostentatious displays of wealth. Of course, it is also a prime location for star watching during the annual Toronto International Film Festival.

The history of the area goes back almost 200 years when the then suburban village was incorporated into the city as the Village of Yorkville. In the early years, around the late 1800s, Yorkville existed as a quaint

Below
The authors Sean Stanwick and Jennifer Flores in downtown Toronto

commuter area north of the city, a role it would enjoy until well into the late 1940s. In the post-war years and into the mid 1960s a metamorphosis occurred that would dramatically transform the quaint Victorian neighbourhood into the epicentre for folk music and hippie culture, with private homes being converted into coffee houses and psychedelic paraphernalia boutiques. Yet even this was relatively short-lived. As urban pressures mounted, gentrification occurred in the early 1980s bringing with it upmarket fashion boutiques, art galleries, cafés and eateries along the area's main arteries of Cumberland Street and Yorkville Avenue.

Architecturally, Yorkville was not unlike many other residential neighbourhoods in the city with rows of Gothic Revival and Queen Anne homes. Today, however, there is a quirky mix of old original and contemporary infill projects, but luckily the original charm of its narrow streets remains. While Yorkville and Bloor continue to be the visible faces of wealth in the city, Bloor Street is about to undergo a significant cultural facelift as two contemporary projects near completion: the jagged masses of the Crystal expansion to the Royal Ontario Museum and the overtly polite modernist glass and aluminium home for the Royal Conservatory of Music.

Chinatown

While Toronto has a vast Chinese population spread throughout the Greater Toronto Area (GTA), the heart of the city's largest Chinatown can be found at the intersection of Dundas Street West and Spadina Avenue. The area is busy with street vendors, crowded with people and overwhelmed with sights and smells. In the 1950s, Toronto's Chinese community was actually located closer to Bay Street, however the construction of Viljo Revell's New City Hall forced the community east to its present location. Populated by well-established Cantonese and more recently by migrating Hong Kong and Vietnamese newcomers, the burgeoning commercial area is spotted with a mix of historic Toronto Victorian and Crown Colony architectural styles. Much of the original building stock on Spadina has been replaced with two-storey commercial infill, several large retail malls and commercial condominiums, although some vestiges of the original city fabric remain, particularly in the residential streets that run north and south of Dundas.

The area is also home to two of the city's most prominent cultural buildings, both of which are key protagonists in the architectural renaissance currently under way. Just west along Dundas is the Art Gallery of Ontario, now undergoing a massive renovation by international star-architect Frank Gehry. And just south is the Sharp Centre for Design at the Ontario College of Art, by British architect Will Alsop. Perched high on its pencil-thin coloured stilts, the Tabletop brings an uneasy tension to the street and the neighbourhood.

Kensington Market

Defining the exact borders of ad-hoc Kensington Market is indeed a challenge, as its edges blend with Chinatown to the east. However, it is generally accepted that it resides just east of Spadina and north of Dundas, its heart, of course, being Kensington and Augusta Avenues. The history and transformation of Kensington Market is very much the history of Toronto itself. In the late 1800s the area was decidedly British. In and around 1914, when those who could afford a better life moved north to the Annex, the area was repopulated by a wave of mostly Jewish immigrants. In keeping with homeland traditions, many established market stalls in front of their homes on the narrow streets, thus giving birth to the delightfully chaotic and makeshift market of today. Although the street names still bear the original Anglo-Saxon origins, the market is still replete with live chickens, fresh seafood stalls and fruit vendors, and remains a vibrant Saturday morning destination for local residents and tourists alike. In fact, the market is so vital in defining the personality of the city that, in 1981, the city bestowed upon it the status of Special District, one of 31 to receive this title.[5]

Architecturally eclectic, Kensington Market is a hotchpotch of two-storey Victorian homes with a few contemporary retail and modern loft-condominium insertions. Over the years, design proposals have been tabled to deal with the aging building stock and traffic chaos including the creation of pedestrian-only zones. Fortunately, these have not proceeded as they would surely strip the market of its livelihood and spontaneous vitality. The market is also home to an innovative prototype for laneway housing. Designed by local architect Jeff Stinson as a response to rising land prices and as an antidote to high-rise urban development, Stinson's lane house capitalises on an under used slice of the urban fabric and has set a precedent for similar projects throughout the city.

The Annex

Bordering the University of Toronto to the east, the Annex is a predominantly residential area in uptown Toronto, defined by narrow tree-lined streets and rows of historic Victorian homes, most of which were constructed between 1880 and early 1900. Bounded by Avenue Road to the east, Bathurst Street to the west, Dupont Street to the north and Bloor Street to the south, the Annex is one of the most expensive areas to rent or own a home, largely because of its proximity to the University.

Residential settlement began in the area in the late 1700s when surveyors first mapped out York Township, but it was not until 1886 that developer Simeon Heman Janes created a subdivision on lands formerly owned by the Baldwin Family, which he named the Toronto Annex. Architecturally, the houses are largely a hybrid mix of the chunky stone-clad Richardsonian Romanesque and the picturesque symmetrical details (towers, turrets and gables) of the Queen Anne period, although there are some smatterings of English Cottage Style, Neo-Georgian and Neo-Tudor homes. Brought forward by architect E J Lennox, this keynote residential style would eventually make its way throughout the city. The Annexe, having staved off developers throughout the years, remains essentially as it was 90 years ago – a tight-knit community with a unique architectural style. The area is also well served by public transport with services from four Toronto Transit Commission (TTC) subway stations (Spadina, Dupont, Bathurst and St George).

Nearby, across Spadina Avenue, are two contemporary projects featured in this book: the avant-garde Graduate House, and the refined Early Learning Centre, both by local firm Teeple Architects. The Early Learning Centre is indeed a polite addition to the city fabric. However, many have suggested that Graduate House was actually the protagonist for the current architectural renaissance as it directly challenged residents to sit up and take notice of the city around them.

Queen West

Queen West is actually less of a defined neighbourhood or commercial district than it is a gritty urban boulevard of 'character' and 'attitude'. Running west from Yonge Street to well past Dufferin Street, Queen West really starts its cultural run at University Avenue, as home to the new ultra-modern Opera House by Toronto architects Diamond + Schmitt. Just west, fashion-forward boutiques, restaurants, and one of the most recognisable landmarks in the city, the white terracotta tile CHUM-City Building – home of interactive media and hub of the MuchMusic Canadian

Above
Queen Street West is a distinctive urban artery, complete with historic stone facades, fashionable live-in studios and urban grit

headquarters – give the intersection of Queen Street West and John Street its perpetual lifeblood. Travelling on past Spadina Avenue, West Queen West (as it is now known in local vernacular) takes form as it morphs itself into the artsy fashion district before it finally stretches itself out to Roncesvalles Avenue and the Parkdale community: a distinctive urban neighbourhood with historic stone facades, live-in artist studios and urban grit. Over the years, Queen West has played host to a number of ethnic groups including the Irish in the nineteenth century, Polish and Ukrainians in the 1920s and '30s, and the Portuguese in the mid-1950s. Recently, gentrification in the Parkdale neighbourhood is slowly displacing the immigrants and artists as the area becomes more desirable to young urban dwellers. Both the Drake and Gladstone Hotels can be found within blocks of each other along this stretch of Queen West.

The Ravines

Other than the rising shore-cliff of the eastern Scarborough Bluffs, Toronto is essentially flat. It is, however, extremely fortunate to be blessed with a vast network of deep, densely wooded, ravines and water courses that snake their way south from well above the Oak Ridges Moraine, past sprawling suburban development and on to the shores of Lake Ontario. The source point for our watershed, these naturally inherited deep cuts are the city's social and natural lifeblood and are as unique to the city as the canals are to Venice. With some at a depth of over 20 metres (65 feet) below street level, the ravines service a number of creeks, tributaries and major rivers including the Rouge River to the east, the Humber River to the west and the Don River, just east of the downtown core.

Above
The city is blanketed by a virtually continuous field of green, as many of the city's urban parks feature tree-lined pathways, cool running streams and bike trails

Although not a neighbourhood by the standard built-form definition, the ravines and valleys, 29 of them in all, function as an antithesis to the glass, steel and concrete urban core and exist as a consistent layer that permeates our interpretation and experience of the city. Providing a natural habitat for wildlife and home to several remnant southern-hardwood forests, they are as much an integral part of the social well-being and physical fabric of the city as the uniform street grid and rows of Victorian buildings. In fact, much of the city's limited early growth to the east can be attributed to their existence and our inability to traverse their spans. It was only upon the completion of the Bloor Street (Prince Edward) Viaduct in 1918 that we were able to jump the Don Valley and finally unify two halves of the burgeoning industrial metropolis.

The union of nature and urbanity is perhaps a tenuous relationship at best, but it is precisely that which the Brick Works project seeks to resolve. Through a campus of restored industrial sheds that will ultimately find new life as a sustainable interpretive centre and gateway to the Don Valley, the Brick Works will holistically promote both the natural habitat and the city's rich industrial past.

1   Toronto Branding Project 2004, *www.city.toronto.on.ca/unlimited/brand.htm.*

2   Jane Jacobs in Cawker, Ruth (ed). *Toronto: Le Nouveau Nouveau Monde, Contemporary Architecture of Toronto*, Maison de l'Architecture, Paris, 1987.

3   A 2006 survey completed by the Beaches Business Improvement Area indicated that 58 per cent of those polled preferred 'The Beach'.

4   According to the Cabbagetown Preservation Association.

5   Larry Richards. *Toronto Places: A Context for Urban Design*, University of Toronto Press, Toronto, 1992.

25 Gladstone Hotel

19 Schulich School of Business

21 Bloorview Kids Rehab

3 Evergreen Commons
at the Brick Works

12 Canadian National Institute
for the Blind

15 Centennial HP Science and
Technology Centre

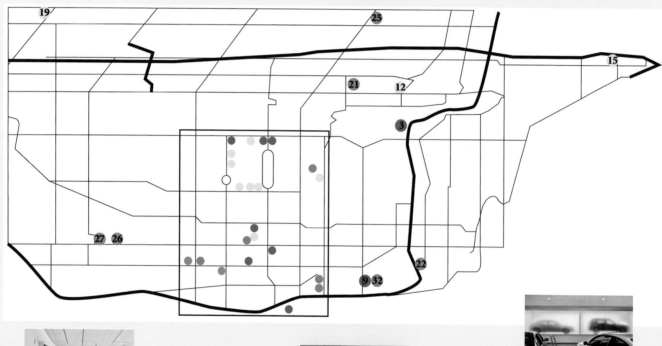

27 Convent for the Sisterhood
of St John the Divine

26 Lux

9 Toronto Waterfront
Redevelopment

22 BMW Toronto

32 Jamie Kennedy Restaurant
and Wine Bar

Toronto by Neighbourhood

2 Bata Shoe Museum

13 Early Learning Centre

18 TELUS Centre for
Perfomance and Learning

6 Gardiner Museum
of Ceramic Art

14 Graduate House

20 Terrence Donnelly CCBR

16 Leslie L Dan Pharmacy
Building

7 Young Centre for Performing
Arts

29 Boiler House Restaurant

10 Bahen Centre for
Information Technology

11 Canada's National Ballet
School

1 Art Gallery of Ontario

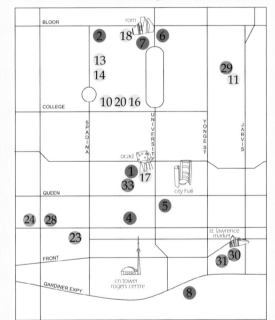

17 Sharp Centre for Design

33 Ultra Supper Club

4 TIFF Festival Centre and
Tower

31 Izakaya

30 Il Fornello Restaurant

24 The Drake Hotel

28 Blowfish Restaurant
+ Sake Bar

23 C Lounge

8 Royal Ontario Museum

5 Four Seasons Centre for
the Performing Arts

Architects and Designers

Alsop Architects Ltd
12 Mercer Street, 4th floor, Toronto, Ontario M5V 1H3
tel +1 416 515 8375 • *www.alsoparchitects.com*

Born in 1947, Will Alsop is an English architect responsible for several unique and controversial modernist buildings. Alsop's buildings are noted for their unusual forms and vibrant use of colour: for example, Peckham Library, London, winner of the RIBA Stirling Prize. The principal studio is in London with satellite studios in Shanghai, Toronto, Singapore and Sheringham. Alsop Architects was partially bought out in early 2006 by the SMC Group and is now known as SMC Alsop.

architectsAlliance
205-317 Adelaide Street West, Toronto, Ontario M5V 1P9
tel +1 416 593 6500 • *www.architectsalliance.com*

Located in Toronto, architectsAlliance is known for its sophisticated approach to high-density development and its innovative reinterpretations of conventional building types. The practice was founded by John van Nostrand, an architect and planner known for progressive thinking on issues of homelessness, and the rejuvenation of underused urban spaces to reshape the city. Recent projects include the expansion of the Canadian Chancery in The Hague and the Pond Road Student Residence at York University, Toronto.

Behnisch Architekten
Rotebühlstrasse 163A, 70197 Stuttgart, Germany
tel +49 (0)711 607 720 • *www.behnisch.com*

Founded in 1989 as Behnisch, Behnisch & Partner, the firm is recognised for its innovative and environmentally sustainable architectural solutions. Its projects include the platinum LEED-rated Genzyme Center in Cambridge, UK, the Mill Street Lofts in Los Angeles, and the St Benno Grammar School in Dresden. The firm has studios in Stuttgart, Germany and Venice, California.

Bregman + Hamann Architects
481 University Avenue, Suite 300, Toronto, Ontario M5G 2H4
tel +1 416 596 2299 • *www.bharchitects.com*

Since its inception in 1953, Bregman + Hamann Architects has established itself as a leading force in Canadian and international architecture, interior design and planning. The firm has a diverse portfolio of education facilities, office, retail, health care, hotel, residential, exhibition and specialised technical projects. Based in Toronto, B+H have expanded internationally with offices in Shanghai, Beijing and the United Arab Emirates.

Diamond + Schmitt Architects Inc
384 Adelaide Street West, Toronto, Ontario M5V 1R7
tel +1 416 862 8800 • www.dsai.ca

Established in 1975, Diamond + Schmitt Architects have received national and international recognition for innovative design excellence. With a strong modern vernacular and a clean material palette, the firm has become a key player in shaping the typical Toronto modern style. DSAI is committed to architecture that is shaped by the life within it and the life around it.

du Toit Allsopp Hillier
50 Park Road, Toronto, Ontario M4W 2N5
tel +1 416 968 9479 • *www.dtah.com*

Established in 1985, du Toit Allsopp Hillier are landscape architects, planners and architects with a particular strength in urban design. With offices located in Toronto, they approach the related professions in the same way they have organised their firm as inseparable and vital components of planning and design. As landscape architects DTAH have planned and implemented urban squares, parks, campuses and streetscapes of all scales. DTAH have a significant body of work related to the key public spaces in Canada's National Capital region of Ottawa.

Eagar + Co. Architecture+Design
487 Adelaide Street West, Suite 305, Toronto, Ontario M5V 1T4
tel +1 416 840 7766 • *www.eagarandlewis.com*

Eagar + Co. Architecture+Design is known for retail, residential and corporate interiors. The principal, Simon Eagar, is a Canadian/British architect based in Toronto, who has completed projects in Japan and the UK. Eagar + Co. projects blend material crafts with practical technologies and systems, producing innovative results. The practice is multidisciplinary combining an architectural 'core' with award winning furniture and lighting designs.

Foster and Partners
Riverside Three, 22 Hester Road, London SW11 4AN, UK
tel +44 (0)20 7738 0455 • *www.fosterandpartners.com*

Foster and Partners is an international studio for architecture, planning and design led by Sir Norman Foster and a group of senior partners. With its main studio in London, the practice currently has projects across 22 countries. Driven by Foster's philosophy of integration, the studio has established an international reputation with buildings such as the new German Parliament in the Reichstag, Berlin, and The Great Court for the British Museum and the Swiss Re Headquarters in London.

Gehry Partners, LLP
12541 Beatrice Street, Los Angeles, CA 90066, USA
tel +1 310 482 3000 • *www.foga.com*

Frank Gehry has built an architectural career spanning four decades. Known largely for billowing and fluid forms, his particular concerns are that people exist comfortably within the spaces he creates and that his buildings address the context and culture of their sites. His work has earned him several of the most significant awards in the architectural field, including the

Pritzker Architecture Prize in 1989 and the Gold Medal from the Royal Institute of British Architects in 2000. Gehry projects include the Guggenheim Museum Bilbao, Spain, the Frederick R Weisman Art Museum in Minneapolis, and the Vitra Design Museum in Weil-am-Rhein, Germany.

Giannone Associates Architects Inc

462 Wellington Street West, Suite 501, Toronto, Ontario M5V 1E3
tel +1 416 591 7788 • *www.giannoneassociates.com*

Giannone Associates Architects is a Toronto-based design firm whose commitment to excellence has garnered international recognition for architectural ingenuity, a rare attention to detail and a unique integrative approach for a fully immersive experience. The firm takes pride in the diversity and wide range of its work from furniture design to award winning buildings and urban design. The work of Giannone Associates has been the subject of numerous publications and has received several awards including six Best of Canada awards, five Mississauga Urban Design awards, the prestigious international annual I.D. Magazine award, three Ontario Association of Architects awards and a special Toronto Architecture and Urban Design award.

Goldsmith Borgal & Company Architects

410 Adelaide St. West . #500, Toronto, Ontario M5V 1S8
tel +1 416 929 6556 • *www.gbca.ca*

Goldsmith Borgal and Company Architects specialises in heritage restoration, adaptive reuse and new architectural works. GBCA brings together the skills and commitment to undertake technically demanding restoration work in order to conserve valuable cultural heritage, while also striving for the creation of responsible and vital contemporary works which harmonise with their environment.

Hariri Pontarini Architects

245 Davenport Road, 3rd Floor, Toronto, Ontario M5R 1K1
tel +1 416 929 4901 • *www.hariripontarini.com*

Hariri Pontarini Architects draws upon the collective skills and expertise of over 20 registered and intern architects whose backgrounds represent a very Canadian cross section of ethnic diversity. Principals Siamak Hariri and David Pontarini have been partners in practice since 1994, sharing values about responsive, high quality design and a strong sense of place and materiality in architecture.

Johnson Chou Inc

56 Berkeley Street, Toronto, Ontario M5A 2W6
tel +1 416 703 6777 • *www.johnsonchou.com*

Since 1999, Johnson Chou Inc has developed into a multi-disciplinary design practice encompassing architectural and industrial design, furniture and interiors, graphic identity and corporate communications – a body of work characterised by

conceptual explorations of narrative, transformation and multiplicity. While the search for 'the elemental' is the defining aspect of a diverse, yet consistent body of work, elements of drama are infused into the firm's projects.

Kuwabara Payne McKenna Blumberg Architects

322 King Street West, 3rd Floor, Toronto, Ontario M5V 1J2
tel +1 416 977 5104 • *www.kpmb.com*

Kuwabara Payne McKenna Blumberg Architects (KPMB) was founded in Toronto in 1987 by Bruce Kuwabara, Thomas Payne, Marianne McKenna, and Shirley Blumberg. The ethnic and gender diversity of the partnership offers a valuable hybrid studio model. This diversity is one of the signature strengths of the practice and has enabled the firm to be a significant player in defining the quintessential Toronto modernist style. The firm is the recipient of nine Governor General's Awards for Architecture, Canada's highest architectural honour.

Levitt Goodman Architects

572 King Street West, Suite 300, Toronto, Ontario M5V 1M3
tel +1 416 203 7600 • *www.levittgoodmanarchitects.com*

Levitt Goodman Architects is an award-winning architecture firm with a diversified portfolio of projects. Principals Dean Goodman, Janna Levitt and Brock James have received recognition for their architectural work in many forums such as the prestigious 1999 Governor General's Medal of Excellence in Architecture, the 2001 Peter J Marshall Municipal Innovation Award of Excellence, and an Urban Institute Brownie Award for best urban conversion project of a brownfield site.

Mackay|Wong Strategic Design

99 Blue Jays Way, Suite 200, Toronto, Ontario M5V 9G9
tel +1 416 341 2348 • *www.mackaywong.com*

Mackay|Wong is a Toronto-based interior design practice with a simple philosophy: to build rewarding experiences for both their clients and their customers. Through a unique approach to design, the firm produces strong concepts that can deliver significant business results through the effective application of brand identity and ideas that are highly strategic and always vibrant.

Montgomery Sisam Architects

197 Spadina Ave, Suite 301, Toronto, Ontario M5T 2C8
tel +1 416 364 8079 • *www.montgomerysisam.com*

Based in Toronto, Montgomery Sisam Architects has developed a reputation for design excellence that is supported by over 30 regional, national and international design awards. The firm takes pride in their ability to build strong relationships – a skill which starts within the office. The firm has been selected as one of Canada's Top 100 Employers two years in a row, as published in *Maclean's* magazine.

Moriyama & Teshima Architects

32 Davenport Road, Toronto, Ontario M5R 1H3
tel +1 416 925 4484 • *www.mtarch.com*

Moriyama & Teshima Architects is a Toronto-based architecture firm with a worldwide reputation for excellence in design. Whether designing buildings that delight the human spirit or developing urban strategies that generate active healthy cities, Moriyama & Teshima strives to maintain our sense of wonder and curiosity. Founded in 1958 by Raymond Moriyama and joined by Ted Teshima the firm has since prospered and built a world-renowned reputation for work in architecture, interior architecture, planning and landscape architecture.

Morphosis Architects

2041 Colorado Avenue, Santa Monica, CA 90404, USA
tel +1 310 453 2247 • *www.morphosis.net*

The word 'metamorphosis' is defined as a change in form, undergoing a transformation. For Morphosis, one of the most influential American architecture firms, this word is the source, not only of its name, but also of its philosophy and practice. Established in 1972 by Thom Mayne and former partner Michael Rotondi, the firm's innovative use of materials and forms have earned Morphosis national and international acclaim and has revolutionised the way architects approach the built environment.

munge//leung: design associates

171 East Liberty Street, Suite 290, Toronto, Ontario M6K 3P6
tel +1 416 588 1668 • *www.mungeleung.com*

munge//leung: design associates has quickly become a leader in the design industry providing cutting edge design solutions for a range of commercial, residential, hospitality and retail clients. The firm is repeatedly recognised for providing fresh hip solutions to luxury condominium developments, popular nightclub venues, high-end residential projects, five-star hotels and resorts, trendy restaurant establishments and name-brand retail outlets. 'Never follow … lead … by design' is a philosophy that is applied and visible in all projects.

Quadrangle Architects

380 Wellington Street West, Toronto, Ontario M5V 1E3
tel +1 416 598 1240 • *www.quadrangle.ca*

Quadrangle Architects Limited has an international award-winning reputation for design excellence and professional service in multi-family housing, cooperatives, non-profits, condominiums and housing for people with special needs. The firm is committed to the notion that design is an evolving process of investigating, testing and communicating. The firm's product is not only the finished building or workplace but also its contri-bution to its site, its users and the city.

Rapt Digital Design Labs, Nicholas Mazilu

1090 Bathurst Street, Toronto, Ontario M5R 3G9
tel +1 416 875 8557 • *www.raptdigital.com*

Rapt Digital Design Labs is a Toronto firm specialising in digital architecture and 3-D animation projects. Working almost exclusively on large scale international and commercial projects, the firm has more recently incorporated smaller scale local projects into its portfolio including the Wild Indigo Martini Bar and C Lounge in Toronto.

Robbie/Young & Wright Architects Inc

172 St. George Street, Toronto, Ontario M5R 2M7
tel +1 416 968 3522 • *www.ywarch.ca*

Based in Toronto, Robbie/Young & Wright Architects Inc (now Young & Wright Architects Inc.), has been designing world-class commercial, residential, and entertainment structures for over 20 years. The firm comprises over 100 architects, designers, and urban planners dedicated to creating truly memorable spaces for people. From the USA to the UK, and from Europe to Asia, the firm's success extends well outside Canada's borders.

Stantec Architects

372 Bay Street, 18th Floor, Toronto, Ontario M5H 2W9
tel +1 416 366 0220 • *www.stantec.com*

Stantec provides professional design and consulting services in architecture, interior design, landscape architecture, surveying, planning, engineering, and project management. Recognised as an innovator in the delivery of sustainable solutions, Stantec continually strives to balance its economic, environmental, and social responsibilities. The firm specialises in airports, attractions, commercial and residential buildings, health care and research facilities, community projects, industrial, transportation, water/wastewater, educational environments, hospitality, retail, and mixed-use developments.

Stone McQuire Vogt Architects

119 Spadina Avenue, Suite1200, Toronto, Ontario M5V 2L1
tel +1 416 506 1600 • *www.smvarch.com*

In practice since 1973, Stone McQuire Vogt Architects is a multi-disciplinary practice that provides a full range of architectural, planning, interior design and specialty services. Led by 4 principals and a staff of 25, their projects range from corporate and retail to hospitality and heritage restoration with a specialisation in sustainable design.

Sweeney Sterling Finlayson & Company – *formerly Stirling Finlayson Architects*

468 Wellington Street West, Suite 200, Toronto, Ontario M5V 1E3
tel +1 416 971 6252 • *www.ssfandco.com*

Sweeney Sterling Finlayson and Co. (SSF & Co.) is a multi-disciplinary practice that builds on the strengths of two well-known and respected Toronto design firms: Dermot J. Sweeny Architects Inc and Sterling Finlayson Architects. SSF & Co is known in the design and construction industry as innovators and creators of opportunity. The office is structured around a collaborative atmosphere that focuses on the creation of economically smart design solutions that promote sustainability, environmental consciousness, urban culture and design.

Shore Tilbe Irwin & Partners
20 Duncan St. Suite 300, Toronto, Ontario M5H 3G8
tel +1 416 971 6060 • *www.stipartners.com*

Since 1945, Shore Tilbe Irwin & Partners has provided architectural and engineering consulting services for clients throughout Canada and the United States. Over the years, the firm has been responsible for a wide range of buildings, accumulating experience in government, institutional, industrial, recreational and commercial developments. With a particular focus on sustainable architecture, Shore Tilbe Irwin and Partners remains one of the country's top architectural firms, combining award-winning design with technical excellence.

Studio Daniel Libeskind
2 Rector Street, New York, NY 10006, USA
tel +1 212 497 9100 • *www.daniel-libeskind.com*

Daniel Libeskind is an international figure in architectural practice and urban design and is well known for introducing a new critical discourse into architecture and for his multidisciplinary approach. He established his architectural studio in Berlin, Germany in 1990. Mr Libeskind has also taught at the University of Toronto where he held the Frank Gehry International Chair in Architecture. In the last 15 years, the practice has been designing and realising major museum projects, public and private cultural projects and large-scale commercial projects around the world.

Teeple Architects Inc
5 Camden Street, Toronto, Ontario M5V 1V2
tel +1 416 598 0554 • *www.teeplearch.com*

From its inception in 1989, Teeple Architects Inc. has built a reputation for innovative design and exceptional service. The firm established this reputation through a broad range of institutional, commercial and residential projects including community and recreation centres, libraries, schools and university buildings. The firm is known for designing projects of exceptional material and spatial quality, with a strong conceptual basis derived from the specific needs and aspirations of each client.

West 8 urban design and landscape architecture
Schiehaven 13M (Maaskantgebouw), P.O. Box 6230,
    3002 AE Rotterdam, The Netherlands
tel +31 (0)10 485 5801 • *www.west8.nl*

West 8 landscape architects b.v. was founded in 1987 by its principal Adriaan Geuze, as an international team of architects, landscape architects, and urban designers designing landscape interventions, squares, parks and gardens. With a hybrid multi-disciplinary approach as a method of confronting complex design issues, West 8 has extensive experience in large-scale urban planning, urban design and landscaping as well as a history of collaboration with world-class architects such as Steven Holl, Rem Koolhaas and Herzog & de Meuron.

Zeidler Partnership Architects
315 Queen St. West, Suite 200, Toronto, Ontario M5V 2X2
tel +1 416 596 8300 • *www.zrpa.com*

Zeidler Partnership Architects (ZPA), established in 1953 and headquartered in Toronto, is an international architectural practice with offices in western Canada, Europe, Asia and the United States. The firm is recognised for design excellence with over 100 national and international awards. ZPA has undertaken projects that cover virtually the entire range of building types within the city. Daughter Christina Zeidler is the Gladstone Development Manager and helped shape the mandate of the Gladstone Development Project in the spirit of urban visionary Jane Jacobs.

3rd UNCLE design inc
8 Camden Street, Suite 300, Toronto, Ontario M5V 1V1
tel +1 416 504 5890 • *www.3rduncle.com*

3rd UNCLE design is a multidisciplinary design firm with a growing reputation for an innovative approach to design for corporate, retail, hospitality and custom residential clients. Its work is consistently acknowledged by the national and international media as demonstrating resourceful, creative and conceptual thinking in the design of spaces that are sensual and memorable. The practice has received numerous awards including Best Concept Design from the Industrial Design Society of America, the Best of Canada design award, the National Post Design Exchange Award, and best retail concept from Cadillac Fairview.

II BY IV Design Associates Inc
77 Mowat Avenue, Suite 109, Toronto, Ontario M6K 3E3
tel +1 416 531 2224 • *www.iibyiv.com*

II BY IV Design Associates was founded in 1990 by Dan Menchions and Keith Rushbrook, both internationally recognised interior designers who combine management and creative skills with sound business sense and a deep understanding of the client needs their profession can meet. Before creating their own company, Dan and Keith both enjoyed highly successful careers working in firms that provided them with outstanding international experience in the design of showrooms, stores, restaurants, nightclubs, exhibits, offices and furnishings.

Bibliography

Arthur, Eric. *Toronto: No Mean City*, Third Edition, reprinted with new essays 2003, University of Toronto Press, Toronto, 2003

Baraness, Marc, Richards, Larry and James, Geoffrey. *Toronto Places: A Context for Urban Design*, University of Toronto Press, Toronto, 1992

Bureau of Architecture and Urbanism. *Toronto Modern: Architecture 1945-1965*, Coach House Press, Toronto, 1987

Cawker, Ruth (ed). *Toronto: Le Nouveau Nouveau Monde, Contemporary Architecture of Toronto*, Maison de l'Architecture, Paris, 1987

Kuwabara Payne McKenna Blumberg. *Contemporary World Architects: Kuwabara Payne McKenna Blumberg*, Rockport Publishers, Gloucester, MA, 1997

Freedman, Adele. *Sight Lines: Looking at Architecture and Design in Canada*, Oxford University Press, Toronto, 1990

Gertler, Meric. 'Imagine a Toronto … Strategies for Creative Cities', a report presented by the Crative Cities Leadership Team for the Strategies for Creative Cities Project, Toronto, 2006

Martins-Manteiga, John. *Mean City: From Architecture to Design: How Toronto went Boom!*, exhibition catalogue, Dominion Modern, Museum of Modern Architecture and Design, Toronto, 2005

Mays, John Bentley. *Emerald City: Toronto Visited*, Viking Press, Toronto, 1994

McBride, Jason and Wilcox, Alana. *uTOpia: Towards a New Toronto*, Coach House Books, Toronto, 2005

Ojeda, Oscar Riera (ed). *The Architecture of Kuwabara Payne McKenna Blumberg*. Birkhäuser Verlag, Berlin and Boston, 2004

Reid, Dennis. *Frank Gehry Toronto: Art Gallery of Ontario*, Art Gallery of Ontario, Toronto, 2006

Relph, Edward. *The Toronto Guide: The City, Metro, The Region*, Major Report no. 35 (Toronto: Centre for Urban and Community Studies), University of Toronto, Toronto, 1997

Whiteson, Leon. *Modern Canadian Architecture: A General Introduction*, Hurtig Publishers, Edmonton, 1983

Interesting Websites

City of Toronto
www.toronto.ca

Toronto Tourism
www.torontotourism.com

Live with Culture 05/06
www.livewithculture.ca

Doors Open Toronto
www.doorsopen.org

Festival of Architecture and Design
www.toronto.ca/fad

Murmur Audio Project
www.murmurtoronto.ca

Reading Cities Toronto
www.readingcities.com

Strategy for Creative Cities Report
www.imagineatoronto.ca

Toronto Building Database
www.towaterfront.ca

Toronto Waterfront Revitalization
www.tobuilt.ca

Ontario Association of Architects
www.oaa.on.ca

Acknowledgements

Writing a book such as this is unarguably exhausting and yet at the same time, wonderfully exciting. Having just completed *Wine by Design*, we were deeply thrilled by the opportunity to document the rapidly changing space of our great city, from the front lines and in real time. Knowing the timing for *Design City Toronto* was perfect we gladly accepted the challenge. Now that the book is complete, personal thanks are due to the many friends, family and colleagues who helped make it possible.

Firstly, thank you to Helen Castle, Aida Krneta, Meghan Brousseau, Kari Romaniuk, Louise Porter, and the rest of the Wiley teams in the UK and Toronto. Thank you for bringing this opportunity to us, and for allowing us the freedom to craft a book that really celebrates our hometown. Thank you also to all the architects and designers featured who opened their doors to us – we literally could not have made this book without your help. Special thanks to Joy Chia, Alessandro Munge, Francisco Alvarez, Antonietta Mirabelli, Robert Graham, Mary Jane Finlayson, Caroline Robbie, Amanda Sebris, Jeffrey Flores, and Kristine Buban – your assistance for this project was much appreciated. To Tye and Eileen Farrow, your continued support and personal interest have not gone without notice or appreciation. A special thanks also to Walter Stanwick, for your generous patronage and support.

To Daniel Libeskind and Will Alsop, your thoughts and ideas are indeed inspiring. Thank you for taking the time to meet with us, to swap architectural musings over a glass of wine, and for helping us to look upon our city with fresh eyes – experiences we will not soon forget

To Tom, there are not many photographers in this city who would willingly take on this seemingly impossible assignment. In you, we have found a kindred spirit; someone whose passion for his work matches our own. Your humbleness belies your immense talent – we are lucky to have found you. Now the whole city can see your talent as well!

Finally, to the people of Toronto … we took on this book because we believed that there are others in the city just like us – people who see the city changing shape and have an opinion about the new form it takes; people who aren't architects or designers but know a 'good building' when they see one; people who walk around the city and are amazed that this beauty lives here. Toronto is full of talented, creative, caring and optimistic people who constantly strive to make this a better place in which to live, work, and play – thank you all for inspiring us.

At the end of this journey, another is about to begin, one that is equally exhilarating. To my wife-to-be, Jennifer Flores, my heartfelt thanks only scratch the surface of my love and appreciation. She has written that it is I who gave her the opportunity to pursue the writing of architecture, but in fact it is she who made the architecture of this writing possible. Constantly challenging and forever curious, Jennifer is the *Design City Toronto* maven and connector; I cannot wait to explore the architecture of our future life together.

And thanks to my mother and late father, who always supported my wanderings in and out of the profession, so long as I pursed that which made me happy.

Sean Stanwick

To my parents Cristina and Eleuterio, you have never failed to support my endeavours and let me know that I can accomplish anything I want. For that, I am eternally grateful. To Mellany, Leslie, Jeffrey, Paul and Myles, thank you for your constant support, enthusiasm, and encouragement. One could not ask for a more amazing family – I love you all. To the girls – Antonella, Cathy, Anita, Ana, Antonina, Wendy, Tessie, Pierina, Nella, Sandra, and Elena – thank you for your friendships over the last 20 years and for listening to me speak on about this book for the last two!

To Sean, what can I say to the person who encouraged me to put pen to paper and helped me achieve my lifelong dream of being a writer. It has been a long and winding path that brought me to you – you are my perfect partner, love, and friend. I can't wait to see what lies ahead. Thank you for giving me a deeper appreciation for architecture and showing me how to write about what I see. I'm so happy that we could take this journey together.

Jennifer Flores

A thank you to the architects and designers for their inspirational work without which we would be surrounded by infinite urban blandness.

For all her support and patience, I am incredibly grateful to Lisa, and to Al and Natasha who in their own ways made this venture considerably more plausible. Additionally, to my mom and dad who respectively think everything I do is great and endlessly in need of revision/improvement.

Finally, a thank you to Stephen Teeple who gave me the opportunity to pursue this parallel field in my early years as an architect, and Sean and Jen for making me part of this great project.

Tom Arban